Along the East
Nevada

An Historical Perspective

Sue Silver

Cover Photos
> Front – East Walker River, near Ravenelle Ranch
>> Courtesy of Georgana Mayne, Hawthorne, Nevada
> Back – East Walker River, near Elbow Ranch
>> Courtesy of Georgana Mayne, Hawthorne, Nevada

Cover Design
> Georgana Mayne, Hawthorne, Nevada

Interior Title Page Photo
> East Walker River, Near the Hot Springs
>> Courtesy of Georgana Mayne

Along the East Walker River, Nevada
An Historical Perspective

Researched, Compiled and Written
> by Sue Silver

Disclaimer: *It is hoped that this work will help to illustrate the activities that occurred along the East Walker River, beginning at The Elbow and following the river north toward Yerington, from the earliest period of the State's development. While much research has been done to produce this book, much more research will undoubtedly reveal more about the history of this area.*

DEDICATION

This book is dedicated to the brave, hearty and "whole-souled" pioneer citizens who tamed the wilderness landscape of the West and whose lives graced the earliest years of the stations and ranches along the East Walker River. Throughout historic times, this area was within what was known as the Territory of Utah, Territory of Nevada, State of Nevada and in the counties of Esmeralda, Mineral and Lyon.

This book is also dedicated to all the early land surveyors who surveyed the lands in this area, for their hard and difficult work in climbing uncharted hills, mountains, ravines and gulches, as they hefted their packs of equipment over the formidable landscape and forded the rivers and streams of this once harsh and forbidding area.

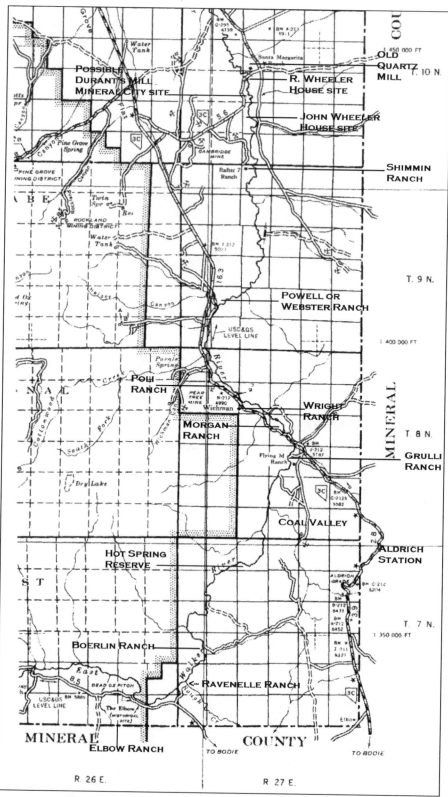

Route from Elbow Ranch to Durant's Mill

CONTENTS

ACKNOWLEDGMENTS

In a work such as this, a vast number of people and earlier works contribute to the knowledge base that emerges as a result. In this instance, people of the past, such as J. Ross Browne, Edwin A. Sherman, John G. Booker, and untold others, especially the editors and publishers of the early newspapers, were the greatest contributors. I was and am humbled by their dedicated efforts.

More recent contributors are the people of Mineral County who have helped to support the work of learning about the enormous and varied history of a place that has endured numerous changes in name and area of interest. When historical documents reside in four differing counties – Mono County, California; Esmeralda County, Nevada; Lyon County, Nevada, and Mineral County, Nevada – it is, to say the least, difficult to adequately access the early records. I would like to thank the County Recorders of the above named counties for any assistance they have lent.

The support and assistance of Georgana Mayne, director of the Mineral County Museum has always been phenomenal. Her understanding that little of the county's history has been gathered together in one place, has allowed these types of efforts to go forward. As my supervisor at the Museum, she has acted as a resource, a sounding board and a friend in history.

I am indebted to others interested in Nevada's varied history, such as Fred Frampton, U.S. Forest Service Archaeologist; Robert E. Stewart, BLM (retired), author and historian, and Cliff Shaw, USFS (retired) and author, who over the past several years have shared email "discussions" about the history of Esmeralda and Mineral counties.

Finally, to former Mineral County Auditor and Recorder, J. J. Connelly (deceased), and his son-in-law, the late Efton F. Swindler, my gratitude for their preservation of the 1864 map of Mineral City, Esmeralda County, Nevada. The discovery of the existence of this map prompted the research from which this book is the result.

A Note from the Author

The ranches discussed herein played an important role in Nevada's history. The men and women who chose these lands recognized the value of the locations they selected to settle. The East Walker River played a pivotal role in the selection of these lands for their ranches and farms.

Today, the current owners also value their lands and their desire to prohibit trespassing on their premises should be respected. It is hoped that those who may wish to follow the route of the ranches discussed in this book, will respect the private property rights of those in possession of the ranches today.

Sue Silver
Summer 2013

INTRODUCTION

There are two branches of the Walker River. The West Fork, or West Walker River, meanders into Nevada from California running northerly and easterly until it reaches Wellington, in Lyon County. From Wellington it again meanders northerly and easterly until it flows through Wilson Canyon to the southern end of Mason Valley. From there it veers north to its confluence with the East Fork or East Walker River, near the site of Nordyke, south of the town of Mason. At that point it becomes the Walker River, which continues to flow until it reaches Walker Lake, in Mineral County.

The East Fork or East Walker River also meanders into Nevada from California, north and east from Bridgeport in Mono County, until it reaches Sweetwater Creek, a tributary, the confluence occurring south of the Sweetwater Ranch that was first settled in 1859 by Irish immigrant Henry Williams.

From there the East Walker River continues flowing easterly along the foothills of several low mountains. The road leading from present Hwy 338 generally follows the same route as the original road that began as a toll road in 1861. It carried freight and passengers to and from Carson City and the new mining town of Aurora, then in Mono County, California, but later determined to be in the Territory of Nevada. Like on almost all early roads, toll stations and way stations emerged up along the way.

This book follows the road that first tracked the East Walker River as it ran north toward the south end of Mason Valley, and discusses some of the history of the early places that were established along the way and the people and families who lived along its banks.

The route begins at the Elbow Ranch, one of the earliest stations to be established after the mines at Aurora were discovered in August of 1860, and located about five miles east of the confluence of Sweetwater Creek and the East Walker River. From the Elbow Ranch, other ranches and farms that were established along the East Walker River are detailed.

Because the river runs from south to north along the route discussed here, early accounts using the term "below" generally meant "downstream from" or north rather than south. Likewise, the term "above," was generally intended to mean "upstream from" or south.

The information provided here is by no means a complete rendition of the property histories and ownerships, but should provide a good starting place for future researchers.

Chapter 1

Elbow Ranch
(Est. ca. 1861, in Section 36, T6N R26E, M.D.M.)

The East Fork of Walker River, early on called the east fork or east branch of "Walker's river," flows northeasterly from Bridgeport, in Mono County, to just below Sweetwater, near the intersection of today's Highway 338 and the Hawthorne to Sweetwater Road, northwest of the historic Nine Mile Ranch. This was among the earliest areas settled in Nevada after the discovery of the Comstock Lode in 1859 in what became Storey County, and a year later, in 1860, with the mineral discoveries at Aurora, in what became Esmeralda County.

Some of the lesser known places identified with, and that contributed to the early settlement of what was northwestern Esmeralda County (later Mineral and now Lyon County), are discussed in this work, beginning with the Elbow Ranch, where the river bends, forming what is called The Elbow.

The existence of the Elbow Ranch on the East Walker River was first mentioned in April of 1861, in relation to the toll road of Clayton, Pugh & Company. At that time it was the location of the only toll collected on the new toll road that was built to take advantage of the traffic flowing to and from the new Esmeralda mines, at Aurora. (Daily *Alta California*, 4/14/1861)

On April 24, 1861, the State of California enacted the law creating the new County of Mono, in which the town of Aurora was believed to

1

lie within, and the town was thereafter the first county seat of the new county's government. (*Statutes of California*, Twelfth Session, 1861, Chap. CCXXXIII, Approved April 24, 1861, pp. 235-238)

In May of 1861, a "New District" for mining had been formed and was described as having "been discovered and organized at or near the Elbow Ranch, seventy-nine miles from Carson, on the Esmeralda road." It was reported that "flattering prospects" had been found and that new discoveries were "daily being made," leading some to believe that one day the whole of the area between Virginia City and Aurora "would be but one mining camp." (*Mining and Scientific Press*, 5/11/1861, p. 6)

In the minutes of the Board of Supervisors of Mono County of June 13, 1861, the Board established the townships of the county, as well as the election precincts. In Township No. 1, the supervisors established polling precincts at Aurora and "one at the 'Elbow Ranch'." Dr. J. W. Pugh was appointed as Inspector at the Elbow Ranch precinct and a Mr. "Dixon" and an Adam Moore were appointed as poll judges. (Minutes, Mono County Board of Supervisors, 6/13/1861, unnumbered pp. 3-4)

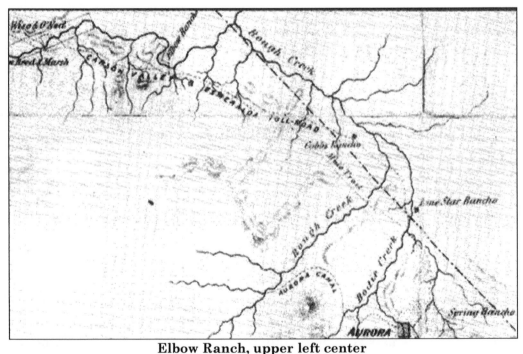

Elbow Ranch, upper left center
(J. E. Clayton's *Map of Mono and Esmeralda*; ca. Feb. 1861, courtesy of Mark Davis)

The above shows the ranch on the Carson Valley & Esmeralda Toll Road of Clayton, Pugh and Company.

While Aurora enjoyed an influx of population during this time, the Nevada Territorial Census, taken in this year, revealed that along "the East Fork of Walker River and the West slope of the Wassak [sic] Mountains," only 150 persons were counted as inhabiting this area. (San Francisco *Bulletin*, 8/28/1861)

By December of 1861, the road which ran through the Elbow Ranch also veered northerly, following the river where mills were being erected along its banks. (Daily *Alta California*, 4/14/1861; San Francisco *Bulletin*, 12/12/1861) In late January, 1862, a terrific rain storm visited the area of Aurora and its vicinity. As a result, it was reported that the "toll-road leading down the ravine [from Aurora] toward Carson was badly washed away. Marshe's House, at the crossing of the East Walker River [west of the Elbow Ranch], was swept away; also, O'Niel's on the river below, and the toll-house at Elbow Ranch..." (San Francisco *Bulletin*, 2/1/1862)

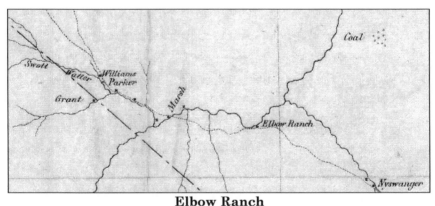

Elbow Ranch
(Map of the Public Surveys of Nevada Territory, 1862)

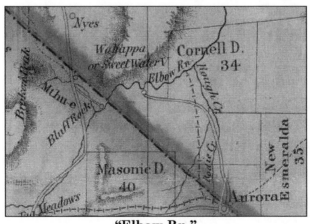

"Elbow Rn."
(DeGroot's Map of Nevada Territory; Holt, 1863)

At the first meeting of the newly formed Esmeralda County Board of Commissioners, in Nevada Territory, the Board established the boundaries of the three townships in September of 1863. The boundary of Township No. 1 was described beginning at a point "on the line between the State of California and the Territory of Nevada where said line crosses the East Walker River, thence down the middle of said East Walker River in a northeasterly direction to a point Known as the Cotton Woods where the Wagon Road from Aurora to East Walker River District crosses said River..." This boundary included the area of the Elbow Ranch and others established along the river between Sweetwater and the Elbow. (Minutes, Esmeralda County Board of Commissioners, 9/29/1863, p. 1) The crossing of the river may have been at or near the location of what was later known as the Morgan Ranch.

Other than the toll-gate of Clayton, Pugh & Company, on the Aurora and Carson Toll Road, the first person identified as associated with the ranch near the Elbow on the East Walker River, was "T. W. Gillman," who the IRS Tax Assessment rolls of 1864 noted ran an "Eating House." (IRS Tax Assessment Lists, May 1864) The *Esmeralda Union*, in April 1864, noted the "arrivals" of persons staying at the Merchant's Exchange Hotel. One of those mentioned was "T. W. Gillman, Elbow Ranch." (*Esmeralda Herald*, 4/18/1864)

In 1865, J. Ross Browne, wrote of the agricultural and mineral resources in the Walker River Valley, which he had toured in the fall of 1864. His trip began at Aurora and, following the road north and then northwesterly down the canyon road, he and his party reached the Five Mile House, a way station.

The next place that Browne stopped he called "The Elbow," which he described as follows:

> "Four miles further on, is another oasis in the desert where the road branches – one leading to Carson and the other to East Walker. The "Elbow" is one of the numerous stopping places which have grown up along the public highways within the past few years. A good and substantial house has been erected for the accommodation of travelers; whisky flows inside and running water outside, so that man or beast can be accommodated." (San Francisco *Bulletin*, 2/25/1865)

John Ross Browne, more popularly known as J. Ross Browne, followed the California gold rush of 1849, arriving in the golden state in that year, where afterward he held several different government positions, including as the reporter for the California constitutional convention. In 1864, Browne published *From Crusoe's Island*, a book which recounted his early experiences in the country's newest and most rapidly developing state. Browne's writings were published in newspapers and also in the highly esteemed *Harper's New Monthly Magazine*. In 1860, after the discovery of the Comstock Lode, *A Peep at Washoe* was published in *Harper's*, which described Browne's trip to the mines and towns of the new territory.

By May of 1866, German-born Joseph Schreck, also known as "Elbow Joe," was operating a hotel and stage station at the ranch. (IRS Tax Assessment Lists) Schreck's nickname suffered several corruptions over the ensuing years, being "Elbow Jack," "Elbow Jake," and other variations as people down the years recalled him to be.

In July of 1868, F. W. Schultze drowned in the East Walker River at the Elbow Ranch, when he attempted to cross the river in an effort to help relieve one of "Elbow Joe's cows" that had gotten mired. Schultze's body was later found and he was interred in the cemetery at Aurora. (Sacramento Daily *Union*, 7/28/1868)

Joe Schreck and his presumed wife, Julia, were enumerated in Sweetwater Township 3, in Esmeralda County, on the 1870 federal census. Schreck's occupation was listed as station keeper. The native of Baden Baden, Germany reported his real estate to be valued at $800 and his personal estate at $200.

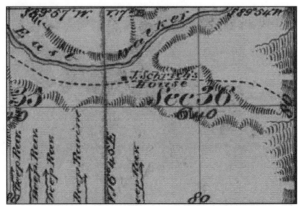

"J. Schrich's" House, Elbow Station
(General Land Office Map, Sec. 36, T7N R26E, M.D.M., 7/14/1870)

A break at the Nevada State Prison at Carson City in September of 1871 set off a manhunt to recapture the escaped convicts. Six inmates took the mail rider, young Willie Poor, killed him and, later, "passed Elbow Joe's station, at the foot of the canon, seventeen miles" from Aurora. (San Francisco *Bulletin*, 9/23/1871, quoting the Carson *Register*.)

In late August, 1873, the "Carson stage with four passengers was coming down the hill at Elbow Ranch, the brake gave way or broke, when the horses could not hold the stage and commenced running, upsetting the stage and breaking it into fragments." The driver and two passengers were "badly but not seriously hurt," while two others were unhurt. "Elbow Joe, as he is generally called, but properly Joseph Stewart [sic], to whose house they were taken," left for Sweetwater to seek medical assistance for the injured driver and passengers. The report of this accident noted it was the first to occur since W. F. Wilson had the stage route. (Sacramento Daily *Union*, 9/1/1873) Newspaper stories in the early years could be fraught with errors in the names of known persons. This is likely the reason the name "Joseph Stewart" was cited, instead of Joseph Schreck, who was known to be in possession of the ranch.

A second article with information from the Inyo *Independent* newspaper, gave additional details of the above incident:

> "Passengers by the last northern stage down bring reports of a very serious accident on Wilson's line, which probably resulted in the death of James Thompson, the driver. As near as we can learn, among the passengers was an old driver, who took the reins and was driving down the "Elbow Joe" hill, while Thompson was on the inside enjoying a lunch with the passengers. By some means the stage was upset, and Thompson, in attempting to jump out, had his skull so badly crushed that it was thought impossible for him to survive. Tom May and George Shedd of this place and a Dr. Cole of Virginia City were among those on board, but all escaped with only slight injuries. May and Shedd remained over to care for the wounded man, but are expected in to-morrow." (Sacramento Daily *Union*, 9/5/1873)

This was not the first serious accident to occur at or near the Elbow Ranch. In 1869 a teamster named John T. Lewis "was driving a fourteen-mule team, with a wagon heavily loaded with merchandise for Silver Peak," and somehow upset his wagon. Another teamster, who was a short distance behind Lewis, found the wagon upset, but did not see him in the dark. He went to the house at Elbow for a light and returned to the scene of the wagon, where he found Lewis dead under the wagon. Lewis' body was taken to Aurora, where an inquest was held, after which he was buried in the Aurora cemetery.

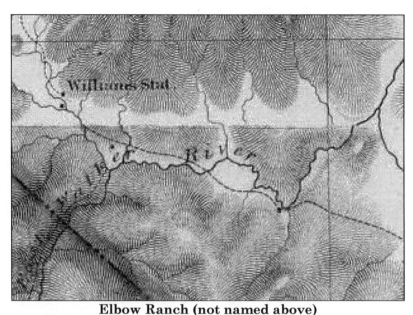

Elbow Ranch (not named above)
(Topographical Map of Central California, with a part of Nevada; J. D. Whitney, 1873)

On the 1875 Nevada State Census, "J. Shreck" was enumerated near the residence of H. Aldrich and family, and before the toll gate of J. J. Welch. Welch was enumerated in close proximity to "S. Baldwin," a stock raiser, who has been identified as Schnedicher Baldwin, of the Five Mile House, between what became Fletcher Station and Aurora. In the Schreck household in this year was J. Schreck (male, age 45, Germany), S. Schreck (female, age 28, Germany), O. A. Schreck (female, age 2, Nevada) and Infant Schreck (female, age 9 mos., California). The census indicated that Infant Schreck had been born in January.

The 1876 Pacific Coast Directory included a listing for "Elbow Ranch, Esmeralda County, P.O. Address Aurora," and named "Joseph Schroeck" [sic] and his hotel.

The Schreck family was not located on the 1880 census in Nevada or California.

In July of 1891, the Board of Supervisors of Mono County approved the payment of $40.00, as an indigent allowance to Mrs. J. Schreck, for the months of April, May and June, 1891. She continued to receive the indigent allowance through December of 1891. "Mrs. Schreck of Clinton" was reported to be in Bridgeport visiting her daughter, Mrs. A. P. Sayre, in the fall of 1893. In March of 1895, the Mono County Board of Supervisors approved an indigent allowance of $20.00 to Mrs. Jos. Schreck. (Bridgeport Chronicle Union, 7/13/1895)

Mrs. Sophia Schreck, a widow, and her family, including sons Joseph (born 1875, California), Frank (born 1876, Nevada), Herman (born 1879, Nevada) and Henry (born 1885, California), was enumerated on the 1900 census at Bridgeport, Mono County. In addition to the sons, living nearby was her daughter, Mrs. Sophia H. Sayre (born 1873, Nevada), wife of Clinton miner Andrew P. Sayre. In all, Mrs. Schreck advised she'd given birth to six children, only four of whom were living in 1900.

The Schreck family remained at Bridgeport until sometime between 1910 and 1920. In the latter year, Mrs. Schreck was residing in the household of son, Henry Schreck, at Smith Valley, Nevada, together with her other three sons. Daughter Sophia Sayre, her husband Andy, and their children, Henrietta and Joseph, were enumerated in the household next after Henry's residence. Family descendants note that the family had lived at Bridgeport until father "Joseph disappeared." (*A Companion Book to Smith Valley, Nevada, A History* (Miller, 2004), p. 179)

In July of 1922 came the news of the death of an "Old Smith Resident," Mrs. Sophia Schreck, on July 20th, at the hospital in Yerington. According to family descendants, Mrs. Sophia Schreck had undergone an emergency appendectomy and died at her home from complications.

The Reno Evening *Gazette* reported Mrs. Schreck's death, writing in part:

> "Mrs. Schreck was born in Germany seventy-six years ago and came to this country when a small girl. She lived in Aurora over fifty years ago and has lived in various mining camps and small towns in this vicinity until she finally settled on a ranch at Smith [Valley] where she has kept house for her sons for a number of years." (Reno Evening *Gazette*, 7/22/1922)

The funeral was held from the Schreck home "near Smith" on July 23, 1922.

Old Schreck House, Smith Valley, Nevada

Oldest son Frank Schreck died in November, 1947, at his home in Grass Valley, California. The notice of his death reported he was born at the Nine Mile Ranch, near Aurora. After living in Bridgeport, the Schreck brothers later purchased the ranch of the Burbank brothers in Smith Valley.

There was no mention of Joseph Schreck or Elbow Ranch in either of the above mentioned obituaries, and nothing further was located about him.

In March of 1880, the *Esmeralda Herald* wrote about a new toll road. The following is taken from *Mineral County Nevada, Volume 1, Mining Camps, Towns & Places (1860-1900)* (Sue Silver, 2011):

> "In the present instance, the Herald wrote that "Dennis Higgins, of Elbow Station, and W. W. Lapham, Superintendent of the General Grant Mining Company, were in town last Monday." The two men had "secured the right of way, and made preliminary surveys for a toll road from Rough Creek, four miles east of Elbow Station, to Kirksville, Mount Grant." Work on the road had already begun and completion of the road was expected to be "in about three weeks." The route of the road ran through a "smooth and almost level country all the way, with no grade to speak of." The distance from Elbow Station to Mount Grant was to be reduced by about seven miles, "making a saving, to loaded teams, of one day on the round trip." (pp. 150-151)

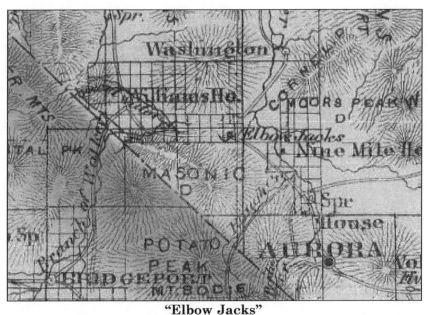

"Elbow Jacks"
(Map of California and Nevada; Holt & Gibbes, 1881)

Dennis Higgins was enumerated at Sacramento, California in the 1860 federal census, but by 1867 was residing in Mud Springs Township, El Dorado County. In that year, he was listed in the Pacific Coast Directory as the proprietor of the Nevada Hotel, in the town of El Dorado. In 1870, Higgins and his wife, Mary, resided on a farm in Mud Springs Township, south of the town of El Dorado. In June of 1871, "Dennis Higgins, of the Emmet Vineyard, El Dorado County, sold 8,000 gallons of wine last week..." (San Francisco *Bulletin*, 6/14/1871)

Dennis and Mary Higgins were enumerated in Esmeralda County, on the Nevada State Census of 1875. A native of Ireland, Higgins' occupation was noted to be "Farmer."

In his subscribed biography as published in the *History of Nevada* (Thompson & West, 1881, p. 421), farmer William R. Lee wrote that he had "located the land where the town of Greenfield [Yerington] now stands." Lee then noted that, in 1873 "he sold said land to Dennis Higgins, and removed to his present home two miles north of Greenfield, in Mason Valley." In April of 1874, Dennis Higgins acquired a federal land patent for portions of Section 14 and 15 in Township 13 North, Range 25 East, located east of and adjacent to the present town of Yerington. It may well have been that this was the location that Dennis and Mary Higgins were enumerated on the 1875 Nevada Census.

A post office was established at "Elbow, Esmeralda County, Nevada," and on March 2, 1881, Dennis Higgins was appointed to serve as the Postmaster. The office was discontinued in mid-June, reestablished in late July, and finally discontinued in early September of 1881. This came about after the completion of the Carson and Colorado Railroad to the new town of Hawthorne, at the south end of Walker Lake, which had obtained the contract to carry the mail from Carson City. Previous to that time, mail routes from Carson City to the south were carried by stagecoach or wagon transport, which was discontinued in or about October, 1881. (*Index to the Executive Documents of the House of Representatives, Forty-Eighth Congress*, 1883-1884, Washington, D. C., 1884; pp. 45-48, Letters to the Postmaster General, Star Route Investigations.)

Bends in the East Walker River at The Elbow

In September, 1883, the U. S. government patented the lands upon which the Elbow Ranch had been established, to the State of Nevada, together with multiple other lands within the State. The proceeds from the State's sale of these lands were to help provide for schools and higher education. In March, 1893, the State issued a patent for the Elbow Ranch lands to Dennis Higgins.

In September 1887, the Nevada State *Journal* noted Dennis Higgins "of Mason Valley" was in Reno, indicating he was no longer at the Elbow Ranch. Dennis Higgins died in February of 1901 and was buried in the cemetery at Yerington.

In mid-May of 1886, the *Journal* reported that "Nels Hammond has located at Fletcher's, the stage station between Hawthorne and Aurora." This was in error as, on August 25, 1886, the Reno Evening *Gazette* wrote that "Nels Hammond who is now keeping the Elbow station on the Aurora road" had a "60 dollar pipe" stolen from his property and had reported the description of the probable thief to authorities in Carson City. A little over a year later, Hammond's daughter, Emma, was married to Richard H. Cowles at "Elbow Station, Esmeralda County, Nevada."

In March, 1892, the *Walker Lake Bulletin* reported that "Frank Hammond of Elbow Station" had sold the station to "Dock Avery of Aurora." Frank was the son of Nels Hammond. No deed between any Hammond and Avery was found; however, a deed between Dennis Higgins and N. Hammond was recorded in May, 1899.

It is uncertain why there was a such a time lapse between when Hammond was first reported to have taken charge of the Elbow station and the deed from Higgins, but on the same day that the Higgins-Hammond deed was recorded, so was a deed between N. Hammond and M. J. Green.

Nelson Irving Hammond was an early arrival in California during the hectic gold rush years. For many years he drove stage between Camptonville and Marysville, in Yuba County. His daughter, Emma, was later born at Cisco, in Placer County, along the route of the Central Pacific Railroad.

In 1868 Hammond was appointed as the agent for Wells, Fargo & Co.'s office at the new railroad town of Reno, Nevada. Not long after, he began a livery and stable business with John Wilson, later selling his interest in July of 1883, to accept the position of farmer and teacher at the Walker River Indian Reservation. For a brief time before purchasing the Elbow Ranch, in 1885 Hammond was a resident of Hawthorne.

The Sacramento Daily *Union* of February 2, 1890 contained a correspondence from "Adolph," a Sacramentan on a trip through the

"Mono Mountains." In part, Adolph wrote:

> "So, George Moyle, the young gentleman who has the contract for carrying the United States mail between the two capital B's [Bodie and Bridgeport], got a pair of leaders for his gallant sorrels, and we started on a trip that covered over fifty miles, interspersed with pleasant incidents, an occasional tip-over (devoid of serious accident), a stop for rest and refreshment at Hank's [Hank Blanchard's toll house on the Bodie and Stateline Toll Road], four miles from Bodie, a night's stay at Hammond's on the bank of East Walker River, were [sic] we were royally entertained by Mrs. Hammond and her portly husband.
>
> Not so tall as F. A. Peachy of Los Angeles, Hammond weighs more than the former, and has passed Tuffly of Carson, and weighs 357 pounds! He rides on horseback, cares for his stock, and attends to the other farm and inn-keeper's duties without being apparently incommoded by the extra weight with which he loaded. Next to this valley, the situation at Hammond's is the most picturesque of any we have seen in this wild mountain region. We leave this hospitable home with regret, and with a refreshed feeling of satisfaction, induced by good food, daintily prepared and elegantly served, a sound sleep in clean and warm beds, for which the price charged was wholly inadequate for the service rendered..."

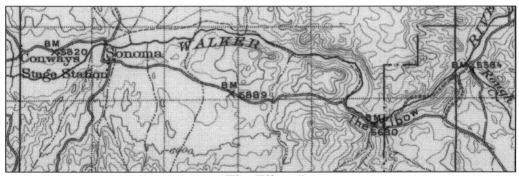

"The Elbow"
(USGS Bridgeport Quadrangle, 1893)

Hammond appears to have continued his work at the Reservation while he was in ownership of the Elbow Ranch, resigning from his

Reservation duties in 1893. His resignation came just a few months before his death on April 19, 1894, in San Francisco. Hammond was survived by his wife, daughter, Mrs. Richard Cowles of Wadsworth, and son Frank Hammond. Nels Hammond was buried in the Fraternal Cemetery at Wadsworth, Nevada.

Amos Green
(from Mary Gilmore)

At the time of Hammond's death, the Elbow Ranch was under the ownership of Manford J. Green. M. J. Green was the son of Amos Green and Green's second wife, Sybil Leavitt. His father was also the patriarch of the George Augustus Green family, of the nearby Nine Mile Ranch. A native of New Hampshire, Amos Green had gone to California in 1849 and mined in Mariposa County before returning home to take his family to the new state.

In 1852, the Green's were enumerated in the California census and were residing in Yuba County. By the time of Manford's birth in October, 1861, the family was residing on Amos Green's farm at Oregon House, in Foster Bar Township, Yuba County, where they had been enumerated on the 1860 federal census. George A. Green was living at Hansonville, in New York Township in the same county, where he was a lumberman.

When Manford J. Green arrived in Nevada is not nearly as clear as when his half-brother, George A. Green, arrived. The latter is known to have arrived 1861 and was later appointed by Governor Nye to be on the first board of County Commissioners of Esmeralda County, while Nevada was still under Territorial governance. He was married to Sarah E. White in September of 1865, in Esmeralda County. In 1866, Geo. A. Green was assessed taxes at "Sweetwater Mill," where the Internal Revenue Service agent noted he was a hotel keeper. Green's mill and house, located on the east side of the Aurora and Carson Road, near Sweetwater, were surveyed in March of 1870.

The Green family members were enumerated on the 1870 census for Pine Grove, in Rockland Township, Esmeralda County, although it is uncertain who gave the enumerator the information on the family, so much of it was in error. "Geo. Green" was identified as being a

"Miller" by trade and if it were not for the existence of his half-brothers, "August" and "Manfred" Green who resided in the dwelling enumerated next after George's house, it might have been difficult to confirm this was the Green family from California.

By 1875, Manford, his mother Sybil and brother, Augustus W. Green were residing in Pine Grove Township, Esmeralda County, near the farm of W. A. Spragg. Mrs. Green was enumerated on the 1880 census at Pine Grove and was noted to be farming. The 51 year old divorced woman's sons were not found with their mother, although her stepson, Everett A. Green was residing nearby. Oddly, the areas of the Nine Mile Ranch and the Elbow Ranch appear not to have been enumerated at all in 1880, and many of the Green family are not found on the census rolls.

By 1900, Manford and mother Sybil were living on the Elbow Ranch, which was noted to be a mortgaged property. The 33 year old was farming on the old Elbow Ranch on the "Aurora Road."

In 1901, M. J. Green "of Elbow Station," sold the property "commonly known as and called The Elbow Ranch," to Nelson Peterson, a 61 year old native of Denmark who in 1900 lived on the George Atcheson ranch, near Sweetwater. The *Walker Lake Bulletin* of May 1, 1901, reported that Peterson had purchased the "Elbow ranch, Sweetwater." From deed records George Atcheson may have taken a mortgage from Peterson, as Peterson gave him a deed in May of 1901 and received a deed for the property back from Atcheson in April of 1902.

"Peterson's House" was noted on a General Land Office map from a survey performed in June and July, 1901, but that location was north of the Elbow, in Section 17, T7N R27E. As no land patent has ever been issued for this section, it appears that Peterson may only have held a possessory interest in the Section 17 lands, but never filed to obtain the land patent.

Little is known of Peterson. No deed was found in Nelson Peterson's name transferring the ownership of the Elbow Ranch property to a later grantee. A deed between a Martin Peterson to Charles E. Mack and George S. Green, son of George A. Green, was located, which transferred ownership of the property "commonly known as Elbow Ranch and all water rights appurtenant thereto," in November of 1910. Martin Peterson may have been a brother or son of Nelson Peterson and the transfer perhaps occurred after the death of the latter.

By this time, George S. Green, formerly the Esmeralda County District Attorney was in partnership with Judge C. E. Mack in the law firm of Mack & Green, in Reno. It may be that the partners leased the ranch to be operated by others. In any event, Mack and Green only held their title to the Elbow Ranch for a brief four months before selling it to Frank Yparraguirre.

A sheep man of some note in the mountains of Nevada and California, in 1913, two years after acquiring the ranch, Frank transferred his interest in the place to the name of the Yparraguirre Brothers, an unincorporated entity that enabled the Yparraguirre brothers to operate their large land holdings and sheep herds.

These enterprising brothers from Spain were featured in the book, *Golden Fleece in Nevada*, which, in part, provided the following:

THE YPARRAGUIRRE BROTHERS
Period of Activity – About 1876 to 1942
Francisco Yparraguirre was born on 10 October 1864 in the small village of Etchelar in the Pyrenees Mountains of Spain. He had an older brother also named Francisco, because each of them had been born on the birthday of St. Francis of Assisi. The family called him "Frank" to distinguish him for his older brother.

When Frank was only twelve years old – in 1876 – he left his home in the Pyrenees and travelled all the way to San Francisco, alone. That was back in the days when parents gave their children responsibilities and they grew up fast. He came to San Francisco because his older brother "Francisco" was already there. Years later he told a friend that just south of San Francisco a railroad was being built. He saw so many Chinamen there he wondered if possibly the ship he came on had taken him to the wrong country.

That was in the day of individual independence – before creeping Socialism gave birth to "The Welfare State." Winter was casting its shadow of dark days upon the land so Frank, young as he was – only twelve years old – took a job herding sheep along the San Joaquin River. That was a job he knew how to do as he had tended sheep in the Pyrenees from the time he was old enough to walk and give orders to a sheep dog.

The next summer, in 1877, the sheep Frank was herding were taken to the high Sierra in the Mammoth Lake area, northwest of Bishop, California, and Frank went along with the sheep. How little the lad knew that someday that same general area would range thousands of sheep owned by himself and his brothers...

Young Frank was not the "wage-earning type" so four years later, in 1886, when he was twenty-two years old, he went into the sheep business for himself. He had been taking sheep instead of money for his wages until he had enough for a small herd. He talked his brother Pablo into joining him as a partner. Pablo had been saving his money and so was able to buy sheep to enlarge the herd. They adopted the Y.B. as their brand. Expenses were low. They owned no land and paid no taxes. One brother herded the sheep. The other brother was the camptender. They were "tramp sheepmen" in the general vicinity of Six Mile Creek near Tuscarora. That was cattle country in those days, and the life of a tramp sheepman was tough and perilous. The brothers worked south toward more friendly people, and more open free range areas...

These thrifty brothers, however, kept their expenses down and weathered through until, in 1898, two other brothers joined the outfit and formed the partnership known in later years as Yparraguirre Brothers – Frank, Pablo, Francisco and Leon. They had been tramp sheepmen long enough. It was time to settle down in one area and build an empire. They bought the Sweetwater Ranch in Mono [sic] County, California, south of Wellington, Nevada, and then began appropriating springs on the public domain in Nevada for spring and fall range. Most of their sheep were summered in the Sierra in the general area of Bridgeport and Mono Lake. They spent most of the year, however, in Nevada. Their sheep came to know the desert hills and valleys around Hawthorne, Luning and Mina. They wintered as far east as Tonopah and Goldfield...

In 1924, after 26 years of operation, the partnership of four brothers split up and sold the home ranch at Sweetwater. Frank took his share of the sheep and ran them as a separate outfit in the same locality for eighteen years, until 1942, when he sold out. He and his wife Josephine came to Reno and bought an apartment house at Wells and Roberts Street where he lived until his death on 28 January 1968 at the age of 103. When he died he was three weeks older than the State of Nevada. He left two sons, Frank and Ramon, and one daughter, Juanita, who married Fred Dangberg of Minden. He left six grandchildren and seven great grandchildren.

In Reno there are three Parraguirre (the Y has been dropped) lawyers – three brothers, Lorin, Paul and David who are Frank Yparraguirre's grand nephews, being grandsons of his brother Leon. These three lawyers, who are still quite young, say they want nothing to do with sheep...." (*Golden Fleece in Nevada*, Clel Georgetta, 1969, Venture Publishing Company, Ltd., Reno, Nevada)

In late December of 1927, W. F. Dressler and Maria Yparraguirre transferred the Elbow Ranch to Bodie Tom, a Chinese man who had worked in the area for several years. It is not certain when Tom first arrived on the scene, as so many of the names of the Chinese residents underwent changes, either in spelling or in actuality, over the years.

The 1910 federal census enumerated "Ah Tom", a 45 year old Chinese man living on the "Aurora & Sweetwater Road," where he worked as a "Wood Chopper" in the mountains. Ah Tom reported he had come to the U. S. in 1883 and remained as an Alien resident. An attempt to identify this man named Ah Tom on the 1900 federal census located a 44 year old Ah Tom living in Carson City. He was the only "Ah Tom" enumerated in Nevada in that year. The Carson City Ah Tom was a single man who had come to the U.S. in 1870.

Again to the 1910 census, the Esmeralda County Ah Tom was residing with his wife, Ida Tom, a young Indian woman of whom he had married about four years prior. Also with the couple in 1910 were step-daughters Minnie Tom, Jennie Tom and Maggie Tom, ages four years, three years and one year old, respectively.

The 1920 census enumerated "China Tom" living in Nine Mile Valley, Sweetwater Precinct, Mineral County. In Tom's household were wife Ida Tom, step-daughters Mamie Tom and Nettie Tom, sons Henry Tom (aged 8 years), Johnny Tom (aged 4 years) and Baby Tom (aged 1 year), and daughter Lillie Tom (aged 5 years). In this census, "China Tom" was also a "Woodcutter" and noted he cut "Pine wood."

The birthplace of the father of Mamie and Nettie Tom was listed as Nevada and the birthplace of the father of the latter four Tom children was identified as China. This confirms that the latter were the children of "China Tom" and his Indian wife, Ida, and that the daughters enumerated in 1910, were not Tom's natural children.

It was the 1930 federal census that first identified this man by the name "Bodie Tom." Although in this year Silas Smith, an Indian man, was listed as the head of this household, Smith was a "farm laborer" and Bodie Tom was a farmer, which generally denoted an ownership interest in the place of abode. The 80 year old Bodie Tom stated he had come to the U.S. in 1870 and continued to be an Alien resident. Neither his wife, Ida, nor any of his children remained with him at the ranch.

Ida Tom, it would seem, was counted among the Paiute Indians of the Walker River Valley, on the 1920 Indian Census roll, together with her children. Listed as "Ida George," the surnames of the children were also listed as George, they being seven in number. In notation on the line on which Ida was listed, the Reservation agent noted: "Married Chinaman."

For the next five years, Ida George and her children were listed on the Indian Census rolls of the Mason Valley Paiute Indians of the Walker River Agency. The 1925 Indian Census also listed Ida George, but noted, "Died Dec. 25, 1924," and identified oldest daughter, Mamie George, as the new Head of this family's household.

By the 1930 federal census, Billie Tom, the youngest son of Bodie Tom and Ida George, was residing with Dave Conway, an Indian and his wife, Jessie Tom Conway in the Plummer Precinct of Lyon County.

The Reno Evening *Gazette* of June 13, 1931, reported, "Death Claims Aged Chinese":

> "Bodie Tom, the eighty-two-year-old Chinese owner of the Elbow ranch on the East Walker river, died Thursday morning at the ranch. The deceased was one of the pioneers of the old camp of Bodie where he packed wood to the Bodie miners with burros for a number of years before he bought the ranch on

which he retired and spent the remainder of his life. Ill health, caused from a stomach complaint, prevented Tom from doing a great deal of farming of late and he expected to dispose of the ranch and go to San Francisco for treatment in a hospital.

He had received an offer for his 160-acre place and had accepted the offer but did not live to see the deal completed which would have given him the treatment that he so much needed.

Justice of the Peace Gregory and Walter McKeough left by automobile for the ranch when a telephone call was received telling of the death. It was found that death was from old age hastened by his infirmity and no inquest was deemed necessary. Burial was had on the ranch which so long had been his home."

Bodie Tom died intestate, and the Mineral County Public Administrator was appointed to administer his estate. The probate file in the Mineral County Clerk's records identified his legal heirs to be daughters Mamie Dempsey and Jessie Conway, son Billy Tom and another daughter, Carrie Tom. Not long after, appraisers were appointed to determine the value of the estate, which included the ranch lands and also a small amount of personal property.

In 1939, the District Attorney and Public Administrator of Mineral County petitioned the District Judge to require former Public Administrator, Fred L. Wood, to produce an accounting and final distribution of the estate's assets, in order to close the case file, which had been open some eight years. In response to the Court's order, Wood wrote the following:

"Several opportunities to sell the real estate failed to develop when it was learned that the Walker Irregation [sic] Assessments, tax delinquencies and penalties had not been paid for several years, and now is approximately $2,000...It will be noted that this property lies in Lyon County, and I assume by law, comes under the jurisdiction of the District Attorney of Lyon County or its Public Administrator. I vacated the office as Public Administrator more than a year ago and nothing further has been done in this matter as far as I know by the Public Administrator of this County."

As so many years had gone by and, after that portion of Mineral County had been segregated to Lyon County around 1933 by an act of the Nevada Legislature, it is not known who acquired the Elbow Ranch as a result of the botched administration of Bodie Tom's estate.

In an article titled, "This Is The Way It Was Done In '31," the Mineral County *Independent-News*, wrote:

> "A colorful figure of the pioneer days at Bodie, a Chinaman known as Bodie Tom, was found dead at the Elbow ranch on East Walker River Thursday morning. He was 82 years old and advanced age and a stomach ailment were given as the cause of death.
>
> He worked tirelessly for years hauling wood by burro pack train and selling it in Bodie. He accumulated enough money to buy the Elbow ranch, where he passed his declining years. For years he had made his home in the hills near Bodie with his Indian wife but she died before he acquired the ranch.
>
> He had talked of returning to his boyhood home, San Francisco, but apparently realizing death was near, requested that he be buried at his ranch. His wishes were carried out."
> (Mineral County *Independent-News*, 6/13/1966)

Today there is little left to evidence that an active way station ever operated at the old site. Known as "The Elbow," locals and others enjoy the East Walker River for a camping and fishing site. Few would ever suspect that somewhere nearby, unknown to anyone living, is the grave of Bodie Tom, who rests undisturbed so far from his birthplace of China.

Of Bodie Tom's known children, Tom's step-daughter Mamie Dempsey married Ed McCann. She died in March of 1977, her last place of residence being at Schurz, in Mineral County.

Son Henry Tom, who was born at Bodie in February of 1909, died in March of 1967 and was buried at the Schurz Paiute Indian Cemetery. Also buried there is his wife, Christine Conway Tom, who died in 1984. Their little daughter, three year old Joan, died in 1940 and is buried with her parents.

Son Billy Tom, who was born in 1918, died in January of 2003. A veteran of the U.S. Army Air Forces, having served in World War II,

Billy Tom is buried in Carson City. Billy's last place of residence was Yerington, Lyon County.

Daughter Carrie Tom, also known as Cassie or Carrie George on the Indian Census rolls, who was born around 1915, married Andy Tom sometime before 1940. According to the Social Security Death Index, Carrie Conway, born April 12, 1914, passed away on September 15, 1998. She was a resident of Yerington at the time of her death. The notice of her death ran in the Reno *Gazette Journal* of September 18, 1998. Her husband, Andy Tom had died in 1969.

Undoubtedly there may be other descendants of Bodie Tom and Ida George Tom still living in the area, although they may not know of their connection to the history of the old way station property, known as the Elbow Ranch.

Today the lands of the Elbow Ranch, at The Elbow, are part of the Flying M Ranch.

Postscript to information about Joseph Schreck

According to Schreck family descendants, Joseph Schreck married Miss Sophia Gang in November, 1870 at San Francisco. (*A Companion Book to Smith Valley, Nevada, A History* (Miller, 2004), p. 179) Sophia Gang, a 23 year old native of Baden, Germany, was enumerated as a "Domestic Servant," in the household of wealthy butcher, Solomon Rosenberg, at San Francisco, on the 1870 census, taken in late July, 1870.

In the foregoing discussion of Mr. Schreck, he and his presumed wife, Julia, a 19 year old native of Prussia, were enumerated in Nevada on the 1870 census that was taken in late June-early July, 1870. Clearly "Julia" and Sophia Gang were two separate women. Julia's place of birth was given as Prussia, securing that she could not have been Sophia Gang Schreck, who was born in Baden. It is not known what happened to Julia Schreck in the months after the June 1870 census and before Joseph married Sophia in November.

Stagecoaches and freighters took the road from the Elbow Ranch to the Nine Mile Ranch on the way to the mining camps of Aurora and Bodie.

Beyond the Elbow

Several small farms and ranches once dotted the East Walker River, as it wended northerly from the Elbow Ranch toward its confluence with the West Walker River, south of Yerington, Nevada. This is the area referred to as the "Walker River Valley," by author J. Ross Browne.

There are two distinct valleys connected with the length of the East Walker River beyond the Elbow, one lying east and south of Pine Grove, and the other lying on the east side of the Cambridge Hills.

Mining and milling activities also once took place along this river channel, but these met with limited success. Mining camps or towns were also hoped for, since having the river as a water source would have been quite advantageous in providing housing for the hoped for influx of miners and shop keepers.

In *The Valleys of the Walker Rivers* (Matheus, 1995), the author wrote about this area as follows:

"The East Walker area, although not actually in Mason Valley, is an important area. Many pioneers settled along the East Walker River in their little valley..." (*The Valleys of the Walker Rivers* (Phyllis Matheus, 1995), p. 64)

Mrs. Matheus was correct that the East Walker River ranches and farms made up an important area. Being in close proximity to Aurora and Bodie, these places on the river certainly played a pivotal role in supplying these early mining camps, beginning as early as 1861.

Additionally, nearly every early farmstead along the main routes between the mining camps and the outside world served as stage, freight and way stations for those traveling to and from the camps.

Chapter 2

Ravenelle Ranch
(Est. ca. 1885, in Section 30, T7N R27E, M.D.M.)

In his survey field notes for the subdivisional lines of T7N R27E, surveyor John G. Booker noted "Ravnelle's House" as being one of three settlers with claims for land along the East Walker River. This was Eusebe B. Ravenelle, also known as Zeb or Z. B. Ravenelle.

"Ravnelle's House"
(General Land Office Map, T7N R27E, M. D. M.; John G. Booker, 1903)

According to a report accompanying an Historic American Buildings Survey of the Nevada State Capitol in Carson City, in 1875 the Legislature authorized certain improvements for the Capitol building and grounds. Of the fencing for the grounds, the report notes:

"...Bids for the fence were called for, and the lowest, that submitted by Miss Hannah K. Clapp, for $5,500 plus $950 for freight charges was approved...The assembly of the fence, which was manufactured in Philadelphia by Robert Wood & Co., was done by Z. B. Ravenelle, a local contractor. The fence and gates still stand." (HABS NEV-13-5, p. 4; Nevada State Capitol, Historic American Buildings Survey.)

Fencing erected by Z. B. Ravenelle
(HABS NEV-13-5 4—5, taken 1972)

"Zebedee Ravnals" was registered for the military draft during the Civil War, at Springvale, Columbia County, Wisconsin. Twenty-five years of age when registered in June of 1863, he was a married farmer with no prior military service. A native of Canada, the registrar noted under in the remarks section, "Alien Claims to be."

In 1870, "Zeb Ravenell" (34 years, born Canada), Nancy Ravenell (32 years, born Vermont) and John A. Ravenell (5 years, born Wisconsin) were enumerated on the federal census at Randolph, Columbia County, Wisconsin. Exactly when Z. B. Ravenelle arrived in Nevada has not been determined, but, in early July, 1878, a Nancy Ravenelle of Rockford, Iowa, was reported to be a Central Pacific Railroad passenger traveling through Carlin, Nevada to Sacramento, California. (Sacramento Daily *Union*, 7/6/1878)

The following year, on April 22, 1879, "Eusebe Ravenell," a 45 year old contractor who lived at Bodie, in Mono County, registered to vote. "Ravenell" stated that he had received his naturalized citizenship in Wood County, Wisconsin, in October of 1859. This date would conflict with his statement to the draft registrar in 1863.

The Ravenelle's are not found on the 1880 federal census in either Nevada or California. In October of 1883, however, the State Land Office issued Patent No. 1961 to "Eusebe Ravenell," for lands in Sections 5 and 6, T5N R28E. This is an area known to be timber and wood lands on the Aurora Crater, located on the east side of the canyon road running between Fletcher and Aurora.

The Nevada State Engineer's Biennial Report to the Legislature, published in 1911, provided information as to a water right acquired by Ravenelle at the ranch on the East Walker River. On his list of persons with water rights on the Walker River, he listed: "Z. B. Ravenelle, sued as Z. Rabinell: 50 acres, 1885, .80 second-feet; (from) Ravenelle Ditch, East Fork." (Biennial Report of the State Engineer, 1909-1910, Appendix, Water Rights and Priorities as Established by the State Engineer, Walker River in Nevada, p. 151)

In 1900, 66 year old farmer Eusebe B. "Ravanelle," wife Nancy and adopted son, Willie Ravanelle were enumerated on the census between the residences of Kate Boerlin and son, Henry Boerlin, and Manford Green and his mother Sybil, the latter two being at the Elbow Ranch. This location places the Ravenelle's on their East Walker River ranch.

While the State Engineer's report noted that Ravenelle acquired water rights in 1885, "Zebe Ravenelle" did not receive his federal land patent to Section 30, T7N R27E, until August of 1906, acquiring the east half of the west half of the section, which totaled 160 acres. (General Land Office, Document No. 285, 8/10/1906)

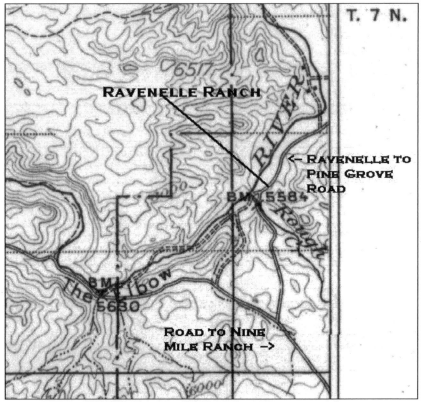

(USGS Bridgeport Quadrangle, 1893, annotated)

On the 1910 census Zeb. B. Ravenelle and wife, "Phillini N." were living on Pine Street, in Aurora, along with William R. Laughlin, a boarder whose personal information helps to identify him as the adopted son, "Willie Ravanelle," from the 1900 census. In this year, Zeb Ravenelle, then 76 years old, worked as a stone mason.

By 1920, Zeb and Philina Ravenelle were enumerated at Hawthorne, the county seat of the new county of Mineral that had formerly been the north half of Esmeralda County. County tax assessment rolls for this period show only the property Ravenelle owned in Aurora, as well as his remaining timber land properties near Aurora. There is no record that Ravenelle purchased a residence in Hawthorne.

On August 19, 1924, County Clerk and pioneer, S. T. Kelso, wrote a letter to his friend Henry Boerlin, who for so many years had been a neighbor of Zeb Ravenelle. In part, Kelso wrote:

"...Ravenelle is still alive, but I do not think he can live through the night. He is unconscious most of the time, and may pass away any moment..."

The Reno Evening *Gazette* published the news of Ravenelle's death on August 23, 1924, writing:

"Z. B Ravenelle, pioneer of Carson and Aurora, died at his home in Hawthorne last night, according to word received by friends in Reno today.

Mr. Ravenelle was a native of Canada, ninety-six years of age, and had been in Nevada from early manhood. He first settled in Carson Valley, later moving to Aurora, where for many years he was in the wood business. He was married in Aurora in 1856 [sic].

In recent years he and his wife had made their home at Hawthorne, he having sold his ranch in Mineral county, on the Walker river. He is survived by his widow, now ninety-four years of age. Mr. and Mrs. Ravenelle raised two adopted children to maturity, but never were blessed with any of their own."

The *Walker Lake Bulletin* wrote on August 30th:

"Z. B. Ravenelle died in Hawthorne on Friday, the 22nd instant, of infirmities incident to extreme old age. Mr. Ravenelle was perhaps the last of the real pioneers of Aurora, having arrived there in its infancy. He was there when Aurora had a population of 12,000 people. He saw it dwindle to less than 100. He saw it increase again to great activity during the Geo. Wingfield regime. Finally he saw it as it is today, with two or three residents. Mr. Ravenelle has always been a model citizen, and was honored and respected by all who knew him.

The funeral took place last Sunday from K.P. hall, under the auspices of the I.O.O.F., of which Order deceased was an honored member. The casket was almost buried beneath a mass of beautiful flowers, sent by loving friends. The ladies of

Hawthorne furnished appropriate music, while the burial services were read by Mr. S. T. Kelso, who dwelt impressively on the life and character of deceased. The funeral cortege was the largest seen in Hawthorne for many years, mourners coming from East Walker river, Yerington, Mina and other places. Mr. Ravenelle was a native of France, aged 92 years."

In 1927, Mrs. Ravenelle became a patient at the Mineral County Hospital, south of Hawthorne, where she died on January 29, 1928. According to the official death record, she was aged 90 years, 8 months and 26 days old at the time of her death. As the widow of Zeb Ravenelle, she was the owner of four Aurora town lots and 240 acres of unimproved lands, primarily consisting of those timber and wood lands that Ravenelle had acquired in and after 1883.

Zeb and Nancy Ravenelle rest quietly among other pioneers of the State, now all gone, who silently reside in the Hawthorne Cemetery. The burial plot bears no gravestones, but is lined with a concrete enclosure with a name plate stamped, "Ravenelle." The plot is shared with the grave of Mrs. Julia Parham, the divorced wife of Aurora pioneer John McKeough and the mother of Walter J. McKeough of Aurora and Hawthorne. It is theorized that Mrs. Parham was the niece of Mrs. Ravenelle, through one of her parents.

In 1914, the County assessed L. J. Wheeler for taxes on the property that was once owned by Zeb Ravenelle. When Wheeler acquired the ranch has not been determined, but it may have been previous to 1907, as Ravenelle was assessed in that year only for Aurora property where he was then residing.

Lee J. Wheeler (42 years, born California) and his wife, Katherine M. McNamara (29 years, born Nevada) and their son Harry R. Wheeler (7 years, born Nevada), were enumerated on the 1910 census living in the household next before Kate Boerlin and her son Henry Boerlin and his family. In the left margin of the page, the enumerator noted "East Walker River." This would place Wheeler on the Ravenelle ranch in that year.

Son Harry Wheeler was found at the Sonoma State Home in California on the 1920 census, but neither father Lee nor mother Kate Wheeler were found on this year's census. In 1930, Wheeler, then 66 years old and divorced, was working as a farm foreman near the ranch of Ambro Rosaschi, in the Cambridge precinct of Mineral County.

On the death of Lee J. Wheeler, on March 29, 1932 at the Mineral County Hospital, the report of his death noted the following:

> "The deceased had spent most of his life in Nevada and formerly owned the Elbow ranch and other properties on Walker river..." (Reno Evening *Gazette*, 3/30/1932)

Despite what the *Gazette* wrote, there is no evidence that Wheeler ever owned the Elbow Ranch, but certainly Ravenelle's old ranch was near enough to the Elbow that some may have believed it was Elbow Ranch.

By 1920, according to tax assessment rolls, the Yparraguirre Brothers, sheep men and ranchers of Sweetwater were in possession of the ranch, which constituted just a small portion of the larger holdings acquired by the brothers.

The Reno Evening *Gazette* of November 27, 1929 reported that, "George Hay, formerly a prosperous rancher of Smith valley, has sold his ranch property at Smith valley and purchased the old Boreland [sic] and Ravenelli [sic] ranches, comprising 1240 acres, on the East Walker river."

In 1930, Thomas and George Hay were assessed for the east half of the west half of Section 30, in T7N R27 – Ravenelle's ranch – and also lands is Section 19, that once was Henry Boerlin's ranch.

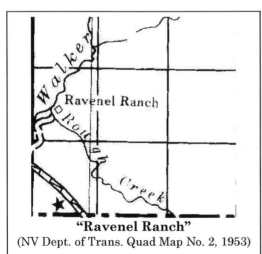

"Ravenel Ranch"
(NV Dept. of Trans. Quad Map No. 2, 1953)

In 1933, the area of the Ravenelle Ranch was segregated to Lyon County by an act of the Nevada State Legislature.

In 1953, the name of "Ravenel Ranch" appeared on a map (at left) by the Nevada Department of Transportation.

The 1958 U.S.G.S. Bridgeport Quadrangle, showed Ravenelle's ranch as "Ravenel Ranch."

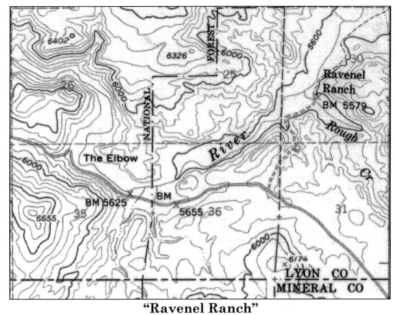

"Ravenel Ranch"
(USGS Bridgeport (California-Nevada) Quadrangle, 1958)

The 1968 version of the Nevada DOT's map did not show the Ravenel Ranch. Today nothing is shown to exist at this location on the current U.S.G.S. quadrangle maps.

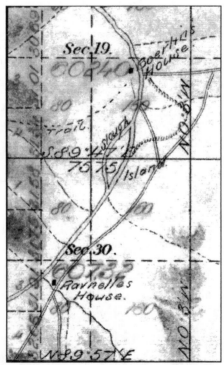

"Ravnelles" House and Boerlin's House
(General Land Office, T7N R27E, M.D.M., 10/27/1903; UNR Maps)

Today the old Ravenelle ranch lands are part of the Flying M. Ranch. Entrance to the old ranch site is restricted by a gate erected on the road between the main road and the ranch road that was once known as the Ravenelle Road. [The latter road was for many years used by the public to travel between the Elbow Ranch to Ravenelle's and on past Boerlin's Ranch to the Morgan Ranch. Unless formally abandoned in the past by either Mineral or Lyon counties, it is by law a public road.]

East Walker River, near Ravenelle Ranch
(Photo by Georgana Mayne)

Chapter 3

Boerlin Ranch
(Est. ca. 1887, in Section 19, T8N R27E, M.D.M.)

In his 1901 subdivisional survey of T7N R27E, John G. Booker identified the location of Boerlin's house. At the time of Booker's survey, the place was occupied by Henry Boerlin, Sr.'s widow, Kate and their sole surviving son, Henry Boerlin.

The patriarch of the Boerlin family in Nevada was Henry Boerlin, a native of Switzerland. Henry was living in the Silver City Precinct, Lyon County in 1870, when enumerated on the federal census. At 41 years old, he was working as a baker. When Henry came to the State or to America has not been determined.

Mr. Boerlin was married to Swiss-born Kate Pfister, who he wed on July 7, 1873, in Cook County, Illinois. His son, Henry, entered the world in Carson City in February 1876. In mid-May of 1876, when Henry Boerlin was working as a cook for Fred Dangberg at Genoa, in Douglas County, the couple suffered the loss of a young daughter, as a result of an accident in which the child had pulled a pot of scalding water onto herself.

Still a baker by occupation, in 1880 Henry remained at Genoa, with wife Kate, and children, four year-old Henry and one year-old daughter, Paulina. It was at Genoa the family suffered the loss of young Paulina on March 15, 1882 in a freak snow slide. Initial reports counted three of the Boerlin family as dead, but this proved untrue; only little Paulina being killed in the slide.

Of this event, the Candelaria *True Fissure* reported as follows:

"Great Avalanches.
The Town of Genoa Partially Overwhelmed by an Avalanche –
Snow slides in the High Sierra at Lundy.
...The residences of D. W. Girgin, W. D. Gray and that of H.
Boerlin were on the next street below Bowers'. Boerlin's house
was completely demolished. The occupants were Mr. and Mrs.
Boerlin, their two children and Mr. Chisholm and wife. All
were buried in the ruins but Mr. Boerlin and Mr. Chisholm
and wife made their escape unhurt. After considerable search
Mrs. Boerlin was found some distance from the original locality
of the bed, nearly suffocated and still holding the dead body of
the little girl, Polina [sic], in her arms. The boy was found in
still another part of the wreck, alive and unhurt." (Candelaria
True Fissure, 3/25/1882)

By March 25th a collection was being taken to aid the surviving
Boerlin family members.

When exactly the Boerlin family arrived in Esmeralda County is
not known, although having just lost everything in the snow slide, it
was probably not long after.

In his report of water rights identified in 1909 and 1910, the State
Engineer identified: "Henry Boerlin, Fletcher, Nevada: 160 acres, 1887,
2.56 second-feet; From Henry Boerlin's ditches on East Fork." (Biennial
Report of the State Engineer, 1909-1910, Appendix, Water Rights and Priorities as
Established by the State Engineer, Walker River in Nevada, p. 151) This helps to
date the time at which the Boerlin family moved to their land on the
river. So do the old county tax assessment records, which did not list
Boerlin in 1887, but did list his property in 1891, although it was not
listed again until 1901, when it was assessed to Mrs. H. Boerlin. By
1904, Mrs. Boerlin's property was valued at $1,430.

In 1892, Henry Boerlin, Sr. died at his residence, near the ranch of
Zeb Ravenelle. He was 63 years, 1 month and 15 days old at the time
and was survived by his wife and 16 year old son Henry. Members of
the descendant family state that Mr. Boerlin was buried at the Nine
Mile Ranch cemetery. Wife, Kate, was living at the Boerlin place as of
the 1900 federal census, where she was listed as a farmer. Son Henry,
then 24 years old, was working on the farm with his mother. Not long

after his father's death, the younger Henry Boerlin established a wood supply business at the old camp of Aurora.

The Boerlin's did not receive a federal land patent on the place until 1905, after the completion of the subdivisional survey in 1901. In 1914, Kate Boerlin acquired additional land in Section 19, T7N R27E.

At just twenty-six years of age, in 1902 Henry Boerlin was elected to be a Commissioner of Esmeralda County. He remained in office past the date of the transfer of the county seat in 1907, from Hawthorne to Goldfield. It was in 1907 that Boerlin married Clara Morgan, daughter of Nevada pioneer rancher Henry S. Morgan.

In order for Commissioner Boerlin to attend Commission meetings in Goldfield, he traveled by buggy to Hawthorne and by train south to Goldfield. An arduous trip, at best, he made these trips for four years, until the time that the new county of Mineral was created in 1911.

In 1908 Henry and Clara welcomed first son, Henry Elwood Boerlin, into the world. In May of 1911, another son, Arvin E., was born to them. In August of 1912, a daughter, Evelyn was born but did not survive beyond infancy. She was buried in the Aurora Cemetery. Another daughter, Clara Arlene was born in March of 1914. In just a few years the Boerlin family had expanded and the children would grow up primarily in Hawthorne.

The State Legislature selected the first Commissioners of the new county of Mineral and, since he was already serving as an Esmeralda County commissioner to the expiration of his term, Boerlin was not among those appointed as a commissioner of Mineral County. He ran for the office in 1914, as short term commissioner and, winning, served until 1916, when he was defeated by John H. Miller.

The road to Boerlin's ranch became a topic covered by the Mineral County Commissioners in July, 1914. A letter to the Board regarding roads in the Mono National Forest from H. W. Atcheson, a U. S. Forest Ranger and native of Sweetwater, was received and filed. The County Clerk was "directed to notify him that the road from [the] Main Aurora Road to Boerlins is Co. Road and to notify Bd in re: condition of Roads." (Mineral County Commissioners, Draft Minutes, Meeting of 7/6/1914)

The road discussed by the Commissioners was the road shown on the 1903 General Land Office map as the "Ravenelle to Pine Grove

Road," that ran from Zeb Ravenelle's ranch, past Boerlin's ranch, nearly due north to Morgan's ranch.

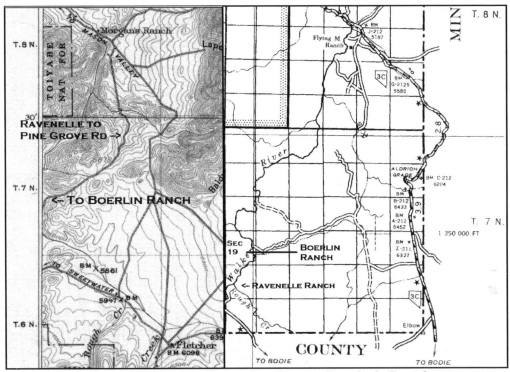

Ravenelle to Pine Grove Road, past Boerlin's Ranch
(Left: USGS Hawthorne Quad, 1909 – Right: NDOT Quad Map 1, 1968)

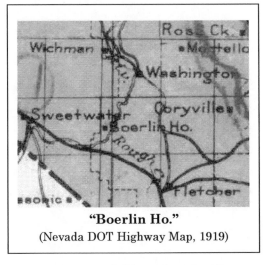

"Boerlin Ho."
(Nevada DOT Highway Map, 1919)

In 1919 Boerlin took a lease on the Miller Hotel in Hawthorne, where all were "accommodated at all hours with good meals and clean beds." In 1921, as a Commissioner Mr. Boerlin worked toward the purchase by Mineral County of the electric power transmission line from Bodie to Hawthorne. He was reelected a commissioner in 1918 and was serving as such in 1924, when he ran unsuccessfully to be the Democratic nominee for State Senator.

For a time around 1926 the Boerlin's moved to Yerington, but kept their home in Hawthorne. Mr. Boerlin successfully ran for the office of

Sheriff and Assessor in Mineral County that year, succeeding Fred B. Balzar, who had been elected Governor of Nevada. Boerlin served as Sheriff and Assessor until 1934, when he failed to be reelected. In 1936, he again ran for the position of County Commissioner, later retiring due to failing health.

In addition to his years of public service, Henry Boerlin was a member of several community and secret organizations, such as the Knights of Pythias and Independent Order of Odd Fellows.

Mrs. Kate Boerlin died in early February, 1933, at her home in Yerington. She had outlived her husband by over 40 years, had never remarried, and was greatly beloved by her son and grandchildren.

Henry Boerlin never regained his health after his retirement from public office in the late 1930s. He died at his home in Hawthorne on September 26, 1942, at the age of sixty-six years. Boerlin's widow, Clara, married again in 1947, to Bodie native Guy A. McInnis.

Views from the river vary greatly

The Reno Evening *Gazette* of November 27, 1929 reported that, "George Hay, formerly a prosperous rancher of Smith valley, has sold his ranch property at Smith valley and purchased the old Boreland [sic] and Ravenelli [sic] ranches, comprising 1240 acres, on the East Walker river."

Like the Ravenelle Ranch and others, the area was segregated to Lyon County in 1933. The lands of the old Boerlin ranch are now a part of the Flying M Ranch.

A Mile Down River

Northeast and beyond Boerlin's ranch was a place that surveyor Booker noted in 1903 as "Peterson's House." Nels Peterson never acquired a patent to the lands shown below, but did obtain the Elbow Ranch after 1903. [For more about Peterson, see Elbow Ranch.]

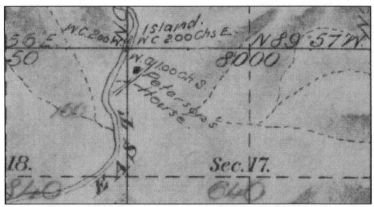

Peterson's House, north of Boerlin's Ranch
(General Land Office, Sec. 17, T7N R27E, 1903)

No portion of Section 17, where Peterson's house was noted to be, was patented by the federal government and those lands remain in the public domain. It is near the area now known as "Raccoon Beach" and as "Dead 'Coon Beach," by local Mineral County residents.

Chapter 4

Hot Springs
Also known as Mineral Hot Springs and Grant View Hot Springs
(Section 4, T7N R27E, M.D.M.)

The area of the Hot Springs is located off the beaten path, less than a football field's distance from the East Walker River. Its location was not noted in the government's survey done in the late 1860's.

Historical accounts of other springs that dried up or new ones that emerged after seismic events have been noted, so the spring may not have existed in the earlier years. It may even have opened up at the time of the great earthquake that devastated the town of Independence, California in the early 1870's, which was reported to have been felt as far away as Bodie and Aurora.

It wasn't until after the turn of the Twentieth century that the location of these springs was recorded.

According to the 1901 subdivisional survey performed by surveyor John G. Booker, the "Log cabin at Hot Springs" existed at the time of his survey. Booker called the spring a "Hot mineral spring." (GLO Contract No. 225, surveyed June 25 to July 2 and July 8 to July 17, 1901, John G. Booker)

In his notes on the General Description of the township, Booker wrote:

> "Three settlers have claims along the river and the estimated value of their improvements:

Z. B. Ravenelle's, ranch $3,000
H. Boerlin's, ranch $4,000
N. Petersons, ranch $300

The land occupied by these settlers, has been reclaimed by conducting water upon the arid land near the banks of the river and those portions of land susceptible of cultivation, near the river have been taken by the settlers...

It may be suggested that the Mineral Hot Springs, located in the S.W. 1/4 of the S.W. 1/4 of Sec. 4, possesses medicinal properties of which the public have in past years availed themselves, and that as a reservation, the W. 1/2 of the S.W. 1/4 of Sec. 4 would cover all the land for which the public might have use in such connection." (BLM Rectangular Survey Field Notes, R0421, approved 1/16/1903)

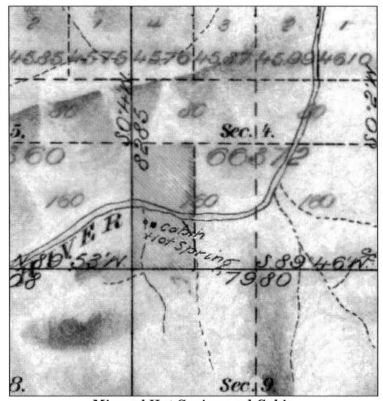

Mineral Hot Spring and Cabin
(General Land Office, Sec. 4, T7N R27E, M.D.M., 10/271903)

In a report on the minerals within the Walker Planning Unit of the Bureau of Land Management, in 1976 J. R. Gilbert wrote of the area of the hot springs:

"These volcanics are altered and silicified as shown by outcrops in the canyon near the "Elbow" of the East Walker River.

"Uranium mineralization occurs in four types of deposits...The radioactivity of hot springs such as Grant View Hot Springs in E 1/2 SW 1/4 Section 4, T. 7 N., R. 27 E., is thought to be due to one of the shortlived daughter products of uranium, such as radon. This is indicated by the fact upon standing, water from the spring rapidly loses its radioactivity (Staatz and Baur, 1953)." (.42 Minerals, Inventory and Analysis of the Walker Planning Unit, Carson City District, Nevada and California; J. R. Gilbert, 1976; p. 126)

As John G. Booker had suggested in his 1901 survey field notes, the west half of the southwest quarter of Section 4, T7N R27E, was set aside in February of 1903 by a Presidential Executive Order. Of this event, the Reno Evening *Gazette* reported:

FOR PUBLIC PURPOSES.
Land Is [sic] Esmeralda County Reserved by Order of the President

United States Surveyor General Matthew Kyle, has received from the Honorable Commissioner of the General Land office, the following letter, dated February 25, 1903:

The United States Surveyor General, Reno, Nevada. Sir:

In your letter dated February 2, 1903, transmitting returns [sic] of survey under contract No. 226, executed by John G. Booker, D. S., you approved the suggestion of the deputy that the w 1-2 and [sic] sw 1-4 of section 4, township 7 north, range 27 east, M. D. M., be reserved on account of the mineral hot springs located thereon.

This office concurred and I enclose herewith a copy of an Executive order dated February 17, 1903, reserving said tract for public purposes.

You will make proper annotations upon the records of your office and acknowledge the receipt hereof. Very respectfully,

W. A. Richards, Commissioner.

The President's proclamation is as follows:

White House, February 17, 1903.
    It is hereby order [sic] that the west half of the southwest quarer [sic] of section 4, township 7 north, range 27 east, Mount Diablo Meridian, Nevada, on which mineral hot springs are located, be, and it is hereby, reserved for public purposes.
    Theodore Roosevelt.

    The tract described is in Esmeralda county, on the east Walker river, and about eighteen miles west of Hawthorne.
    (Reno Evening *Gazette*, 3/4/1903)

The rectangular survey of the township, issued in October 1903, states:

Notice of Reservation.
The W 1/2 of the SW 1/4 is reserved for public purposes on account of mineral springs by Executive Order, dated February 17th, 1903.

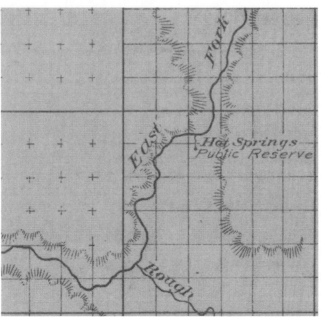

(Nevada Bureau of Mining and Geology, Map of Walker River Basin, 1909)

According to one Mineral County resident, in past years an old bath tub served as a receptacle for the warm waters of the spring and the cabin mentioned by Booker was still standing. The cabin went away around the time that "hippies" invaded the area in the 1960's.

Today the spring has been connected to a stone and mortar hot tub, including bench seating. The actual spring is a short distance from the stone tub and the water is piped from the spring to the tub.

Hot Tub at Hot Springs
(Photo courtesy of Frank Estrella, HighDesertDrifters.com)

The hot tub seats about four or five people
(Author's photo, 2013)

John G. Booker, Deputy Surveyor

The son of Simeon M. Booker and Mary Catherine Cobb, John G. Booker was a native of California who came to Nevada as a young boy. His mother died at Aurora in June of 1867, where she is buried. In 1870, the Booker family was found in two places – at Sweetwater, near the Henry Williams ranch, and also at Aurora. Simeon Booker worked as teamster in this year. They may have been on the road traveling home to Aurora when found at Sweetwater.

The Booker's remained at Aurora for many years after. Simeon Booker's sister, Rachel was married there in 1870 to physician and attorney, David J. Lewis. Both Booker and Lewis were involved in local county politics; Simeon Booker as the Esmeralda County Public Administrator (1868) and Assessor (1870) and David Lewis served as the County Clerk (1870 and 1872) and later as the County District Attorney (1880). John Booker's sister, Etta, was married to Myron Waltze of Mono County, in 1875, and his father married again in 1878, to Mrs. Kate Dulin of San Francisco.

By 1880, Simeon Booker was running a grocery store at Aurora and supporting his remaining family of two sons, John and Frederick, and stepdaughter, Theodora Dulin. In 1883, just a few days before Christmas, the family home burned down and was later replaced when Booker purchased the old Ike Levy house from the Levy & Company mercantile house.

In May of 1892, John G. Booker was "appointed a Deputy U. S. Mineral Surveyor," and advertised the fact in the *Chloride Belt* newspaper at Candelaria. Later that year, John married Mrs. Annie Mooney in Bodie. His new wife was the daughter of another Aurora pioneer, Thomas B. Pritchard, who had once been involved in owning the Big Indian Mine, on Mount Grant. Her brother, Guy Pritchard, was man who later discovered the silver ore that led to the Lucky Boy mines on the old Bodie Road, while doing county road work on it.

By 1893, Simeon Booker was residing at Sweetwater and had been appointed Postmaster in that year. In April of 1896, Mrs. Annie Booker died at Aurora and was buried in the Aurora cemetery, next to the grave of John Booker's mother. Her death left Booker with two young sons to raise on his own.

In 1899, Simeon and John Booker purchased the store of W. J. Douglass, in the town of Hawthorne.

In February of 1901, John G. Booker was awarded General Land Office Contract No. 226 to resurvey the township lines and subdivisions in the area of the East Walker River. He began his surveys on June 25, 1901, completing his work in Townships 7, 8 and 9 North, Range 27 East, in August of 1902.

The Esmeralda County Commissioners, in March of 1901, ordered "that J. G. Booker be empowered to make a survey to determine the county line between Nye and Esmeralda, and settle the controversy as to whether the Tonopah mines are in this county or Nye." (*Walker Lake Bulletin*, 4/3/1901) Booker's preliminary assessment was that Tonopah was in Nye County. (*Walker Lake Bulletin*, 6/5/1901) John was married in Hawthorne to Miss Virginia Moore in June 1901.

In June of 1902, the *Walker Lake Bulletin* reported that:

> "J. G. Booker has just completed a fine map of Tonopah. It shows all mining locations so far made, and is invaluable to all persons interested in the great camp." (*Walker Lake Bulletin*, 6/12/1902)

In 1903, John Booker moved his family to Tonopah to live. At Tonopah, Booker partnered with a Mr. Bradford in the engineering firm of Booker and Bradford. Together, in 1902, the two men produced a map of the town of Tonopah, the earliest known map of the place to exist today.

Five years after President Roosevelt's Executive Order reserving the hot springs for public purposes, John G. Booker was residing in Reno, where, in August of 1908, he died. John G. Booker was buried in the Knights of Pythias Cemetery, in Reno.

Of his passing, the Bridgeport *Chronicle-Union* wrote:

> "John G. Booker, a brother-in-law of Myron Waltze of this place, died in Reno on the 21st inst. from typhoid fever. Mr. Booker was a native of California and aged 47 years. He leaves an aged father, a wife and two children.
>
> Mr. Booker was favorably known throughout the mining west as a successful civil engineer and one prominently

connected with the early day history of Tonopah and at one time was rated as a man of considerable wealth." (Bridgeport *Chronicle-Union*, 8/29/1908)

Thanks to Deputy Surveyor John G. Booker, today the mineral hot springs continue to be used by locals and others, who have learned of its location.

East Walker River, north of the Hot Spring

The public reserve lands are presently under the management of the U. S. Forest Service. The East Walker River is north of the springs within the reserved lands.

Chapter 5

ALDRICH STATION
(Est. ca. 1864, in Section 6, T7N R28E, M.D.M.)

This place is not on the East Walker River, but is north of Fletcher, and about four miles east from the Hot Springs. It is near the area known as Coal Valley.

In 1865, J. Ross Browne wrote of the agricultural and mineral resources in the Walker River Valley, which he had toured in the summer of 1864. His trip began at Aurora and, following the road north and then northwesterly down the canyon road, he and his party reached the Five Mile House, a way station. The next place Browne stopped was called "The Elbow."

Leaving The Elbow, Browne "followed the right branch of the road across a desert valley, some eight miles in width to a range of low mountains which intervenes between this point and Walker Valley." He noted that by "diverging a few miles to the right [east], a much shorter route to Walker Valley could be made; the only obstacles at present being some two or three ragged arroyas [sic], which would require bridging." (San Francisco *Bulletin*, 2/25/1865)

After passing through the Five-mile cañon, the author described the scenery as being "wild and desolate," noting that it also possessed a "rugged grandeur characteristic of most of the spurs of the Sierra." To the right of the road, Browne wrote, "can be seen at occasional intervals the towering peak of Mount Grant – so named in honor of our distinguished Federal General, by Major E. A. Sherman, who has recently made a topographical survey of this region." (San Francisco *Bulletin*, 2/25/1865)

Browne continued to describe his travel along the Five-mile cañon road:

> "Descending the canon at a gradual inclination, its walls converge till they form a winding pass almost perpendicular on each side. Through this runs a narrow roadway, evidently the bed of a mountain stream, now quite dry and covered with fine gravel. I was told by my guides that excellent placer diggings had been discovered in this vicinity. The scarcity of water was the great obstacle to success.
>
> Passing out of the canon, a fine view is had of the Two Sentinels, Mount Bullion and Mount Grant, and of the rolling hills embraced within the intervening range of country, in which important discoveries of coal have recently been made."
>
> It may be well to mention in this connection that some days later I made a tour of the coal district. Several of the veins which I examined present evidence of coal deposits, some of them being as clearly defined as any I had previously seen in Puget's Sound. The excavations so far made have reached only the superficial strata, which is highly promising. The coal is a light carbon, interlined clear with shale and highly inflammable. Further explorations and experiments may result in the discovery of vast deposits of coal in this neighborhood. The surface of the earth for a distance of ten miles north and south, is speckled at intervals with glittering sheets of "shale," which experienced miners pronounce an infallible sign of the proximity of coal." (San Francisco *Bulletin*, 1/25/1865)

As Browne continued on to the "Settlements on Walker River," he wrote that:

> "Leaving the coal-fields on the right, we skirted along the base of a mountain range to the left, till the road struck into the first of series of small valleys lying along the course of Walker river. The distance, he wrote, "from Aurora to the first crossing of the river, I estimated to be about 25 miles." (San Francisco *Bulletin*, 1/25/1865)

In imparting this estimated mileage between Aurora and the point at which he had reached the first crossing of the river after passing the area of the coal discoveries, Browne also provided information as to the approximate distance from Aurora to Coal Valley, that distance being less than 25 miles.

In the field survey notes of the 1867 township boundary survey done by R. A. Chase and Abram Lash, Jr., of the boundaries between Township 7 North, Ranges 27 and 28 East, the veteran surveyors ran the line separating Section 1, T7N R27E and Section 6, T7N R28E noting, among other things, the summit of a "chalk hill", a "basin used as antelope drive by Indian [sic]," a "prospect shaft for coal" a quarter mile distant of their mark, and the post set to mark the corner common to Sections 1 and 12, T7N R27E and Sections 6 & 7, T7N R28E. Also noted was: "This mile over a barren broken country with a few pines and cedars." (BLM R0026, 9/25/1867, p. 174)

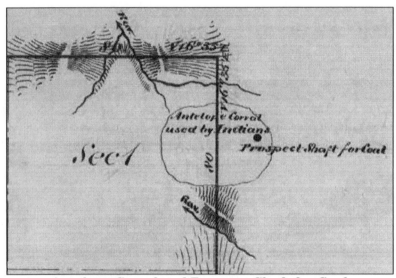

Antelope Corral and Prospect Shaft for Coal
(General Land Office, Section 1, T7N R27E, M.D.M., 1869)

The area to the east [right] of Section 1, shown above, was surveyed by the General Land Office in 1880, to subdivide the sections of the township, with the map being approved in January, 1881. No structures or other features other than a road, were identified at that time as being within in Section 6 of Township 7 North, Range 28 East, immediately to the east of Section 1, T7N R27E, as shown in the following map view.

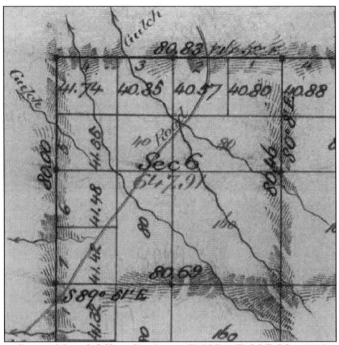

(General Land Office, Section 6, T7N R28E, M.D.M., 1881)

Two mid-twentieth century reports were found that included information about the place they called "Aldrich Station." The first, in 1966, noted:

"Axelrod (1956) has mapped diatomaceous rocks at Aldrich Station (no. 32 on plate 1) along the western border of Mineral County. The diatomite is in a series of shaly and tuffaceous sediments, 200 to 1,600 feet thick, that constitute a part of the Aldrich Station Formation. Plant fossils indicate a Pliocene age for the formation. In general, the diatomite beds are thin and impure; perhaps the best exposure is along the road at the base of Aldrich Hill, where the diatomaceous sediments form a white unit that dips about 40°W and appears to be at least several tens of feet thick. Scattered trenchs [sic] indicate some minor prospecting activity." (Nevada Bureau of Mines; Vernon E. Scheid, Director; Report 14, Industrial Mineral Deposits of Mineral County, Nevada; N. L. Archbold; Mackay School of Mines, University of Nevada, 1966)

The second mention was included in a 1982 report for the Bureau of Land Management regarding cultural resources reviewed for the department. This instance noted the location of "Aldrich Station," citing it was at the "West base of the Wassuk Range, 7 miles west-northwest of Corey Peak," at an elevation of 6240 feet. The site had been recorded by A. McLane in March of 1980, as CrNv-03-1967. The only comment about this resource was:

> "This is probably an early stage or freight station. Needs more information." (American Museum of Natural History, New York; Bureau of Land Management, Nevada; Cultural Resource Overview, Carson City District, West Central Nevada; Lorann S. A. Pendleton; Alvin R. McLane; David Hurst Thomas; Cultural Resource Series No. 5, Part 2, 1982)

In 1909, the first U.S.G.S. quadrangle topographic map was issued for the Hawthorne Quadrangle. Like the 1881 General Land Office survey map, this also did not show any feature within the area identified to have been Aldrich Station. It is almost as if whoever occupied what was identified as Aldrich Station, left nothing behind to evidence their residency there.

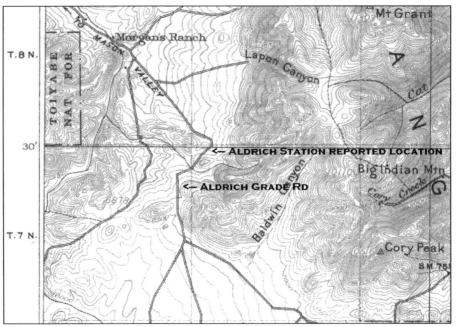

(USGS Hawthorne Quadrangle, 1909; annotated)

In 1957 the U.S.G.S. Walker Lake 1:250,000 quadrangle map was published and included the location of Aldrich Station, as shown in the following view.

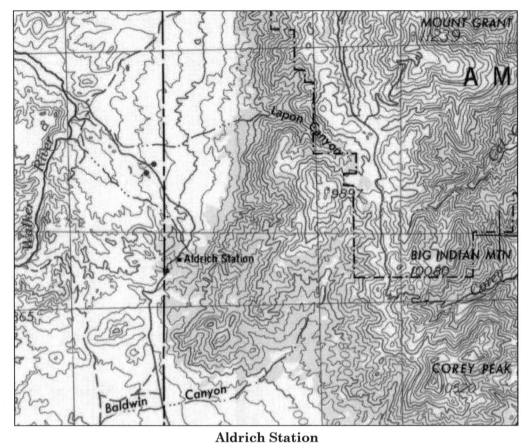

Aldrich Station
(USGS Walker Lake, Nev-Cal; Western United States 1:250,000, 1957 Rev 1969)

Land in this vicinity came into the possession of New York-born Horton Aldrich, sometime around 1873 or 1874. No land patent for Section 6, T7N R28E, however, ever issued to any person.

Aldrich had arrived in the West at San Francisco, in April of 1856, upon the later ill-fated steamer, the Brother Jonathan. A year later, he had made his way to Carson Valley, then in the Territory of Utah. On January 22, 1857, he was married to Mrs. M. A. Cooksey, the former Miss Emma Mitchell, a native of England. (Daily *Alta California*, 2/12/1857)

The following early news item about Mr. Aldrich appeared in April, 1857:

> "From Carson Valley. – Messrs. H. Aldrich and W. Wood, arrived at Placerville, says the Mountain Democrat, on Thursday, direct from Carson Valley. They left the Valley on Tuesday, making the trip in two and a half days. They report

15 feet of snow on the summit. They brought a hand-sled to the edge of the snow (a few miles this side of Slippery Ford), on which they intend to convey to the Valley a stock of boots, which are selling readily at $12 to $14 per pair. The miners of Gold Cañon continue to do well. The gold from these diggings sells at $14 per ounce. Grass is plenty in the valley, and the settlers are busy at work on their farms, with every prospect of abundant crops. A report was prevalent in the Valley to the effect that a serious dissension had arisen among the Saints at Salt Lake City. It is said that Brigham Young has been compelled to flee the city, to save himself from the fury of his flock. The difficulty had its origin in matters relating to the administration of the church property, we believe." (Daily *Alta California*, 4/14/1857)

Three years later, "H. Aldridge," (age 25, born New York), Emma Aldridge (25 years, born England), Nelson Aldridge (2 years, born California) and Edward Aldridge (1 month, born California), were enumerated at Cedarville, in Cosumnes Township, in the southern end of El Dorado County. Here Horton Aldrich was a miner. By the time of the 1870 census, "Henry Aldrich", a New York-born farmer, and Emma Aldrich, born England, were residing in Township No. 7, Mason Valley (Pine Grove Post Office), in Esmeralda County, Nevada. The family had lost son Nelson between the 1860 and 1870 censuses, but had gained son William (9 years, born California), daughter Mary (6 years, born California), son Spencer (3 years, born Nevada) and daughter Capitola (1 year, born Nevada).

The family grew even more by the time of 1875 Nevada State Census, where the Aldrich family was enumerated near the area of the Elbow Ranch. In this year, two more Aldrich children were found in the household, H. L. Aldrich (male, 3 years, born Nevada) and E. Aldrich (1 year, born Nevada).

In 1879, the *Esmeralda Herald*, published at Aurora, reported:

"Mount Grant Items. – A lady correspondent, writing from Coal Valley, furnishes us the following items of interest: E. W. Bennett is rapidly pushing the new road to Mount Grant from Coal Valley. The same gentleman has three mines which are looking remarkably well...William Miller and H. Aldrich have struck a mine that, from present indications, would seem to rival the famous Bennett mine." (*Esmeralda Herald*, 7/5/1879)

E. W. Bennett's new road to Mount Grant was to facilitate the work on the Big Indian Mine, of which Bennett was a part owner. The *Herald* noted he was "the principal owner with Mr. Hamlin of Pine Grove." This same road provided access to the town called Kirksville, that had been established at the mine of the Mount Grant Company, then under the superintendence of W. W. Lapham.

Also in 1879, daughter "Maria Ellen Aldridge" was married on November 3rd to Wilson Cain, at Aurora. Cain had been a registered voter at Bodie, in Mono County, from 1878 to 1879.

The 1880 federal census has been found to have missed several areas of Esmeralda County during the enumeration process. One of these areas was between Sweetwater and the area of the Elbow Ranch, and also the Nine Mile Ranch. Because of this, the 1880 census for the Aldrich family is not available; however, son William "Aldridge" was working as a vaquero and living at Aurora in the household of Jas. Thompson, Jailor. Eldest son, Edward Aldrich, then 20 years old, was a farm hand living on the farm of James Birmingham in Mason Valley.

Five years later, the *Walker Lake Bulletin* reported that, "Hort. Aldrich, of Coal Valley, and William Somerville, of Coryville are out recording claims." (*Walker Lake Bulletin*, 12/3/1884)

In April of 1888, the 59 year old Aldrich had registered to vote in San Bernardino County, California. His was a miner residing in Riverside, which was later segregated to become part of Riverside County.

Nine months later the news of Aldrich's death was reported:

> "A man who has resided in Riverside for some months past, named Horton Aldrich, died at Perris this morning about 9 o'clock. Mr. Aldrich was about 52 years old, formerly from New York, and has a nephew of the same name. We do not learn the cause of death, but understand he was a consumptive." (Riverside (CA) *Daily Press*, 12/29/1888, Saturday)

Sometime after February, 1911, the Bridgeport *Chronicle-Union* reported:

"A Carson company with F. B. Whitelaw as superintendent, is arranging to do considerable work on the coal property near the Joe Mathews place on the East Walker and a short distance from the Aldrich cabin on the Bodie road..."

While the above reports the Aldrich cabin was on "the Bodie road," it is certain that the writer meant the same road that was earlier called the Aurora to Pine Grove road, now Aldrich Grade road, a portion of which was shown running through Section 6, T7N R28E, 1881 per the General Land Office map. At the time of this article, Joe Mathews owned the Grulli Ranch, north of the Aldrich Grade summit and south of the Morgan Ranch.

Mrs. Emma Aldrich lived many years after the death of her husband, when her own death occurred in 1927:

"Oldest Nevada Settler Is Dead at Daughter's Home Here at Age of 86. – Mrs. Emma G. Aldrich, Resident of Nevada for Seventy-five Years Passes Away; Won Silver Cup

The oldest known settler in Nevada, Mrs. Emma G. Aldrich, died this morning at the home of her daughter, Mrs. Hattie S. Ede, after seventy-five years spent within the state. She was eighty-six years old, and at a gathering of old-timers of Nevada several years ago, Mrs. Aldrich was awarded a silver cup as the oldest living pioneer of Nevada.

Mrs. Aldrich has been sick for several months, and was unable to attend the last meeting of pioneers of this state. Born in Monmouthshire, England, on October 7, 1840, Mrs. Aldrich, then Emma Mitchell, came to St. Louis in 1841. In 1852, she crossed the plains, and settled in Nevada, then in Utah Territory, locating at Genoa.

She married Horton Aldrich on January 22, 1857, and that same year, she and her husband moved to California, where they engaged in placer mining on a small stream north of Placerville. They made the trip by pack train, Mrs. Aldrich riding on a mule.

In 1863, she moved to Carson valley where she lived on a ranch, and she had the first hive of bees in Nevada. She bought the Virginia ranch in 1865 and the place is now the

Dangberg ranch. The ranch was sold to the Dangberg interests in 1870. Her husband died in 1888.

Since moving from her ranch, Mrs. Aldrich has lived in different parts of the state, and for the past several years has been making here home in Reno with her daughter.

She leaves three daughters, Mrs. Hattie S. Ede of Reno, Mrs. Ollie Pickett of Galt, Cal., Mrs. Mary Creitzer of Greenbach, Ore.; two sons, Edward H. Aldrich of Galt, Cal., and William Alrich [sic] of Platt, Idaho.

She was a native of England, aged eighty-six years and seven months. Funeral arrangements will be announced by the Ross-Burke Company." [Emma G. Aldrich was buried at the Mountain View Cemetery, in Reno.]

The following view shows the location of the "chalk hill" and Aldrich Station as they have been cited in the various notes and references mentioned herein.

Aldrich Station and Chalk Hill
(USGS Aerial - Ninemile Quadrangle, 2000)

The road leading to the lower left corner of the previous photo image led to the Ravenelle and Boerlin ranches, on the East Walker River and was known as the Ravenelle and Pine Grove Road.

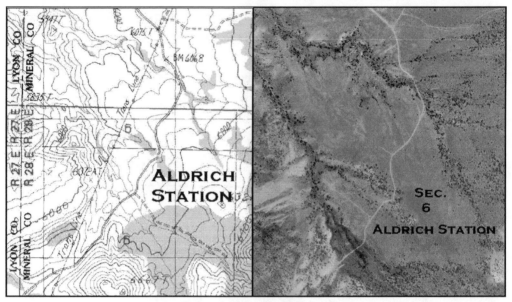

Site of Aldrich Station
(USGS Ninemile Quadrangle, 1988 (Topo) and 2000 (Aerial))

The history of the place now known as the site of Aldrich Station has not revealed that it was used as a stage, freight or way station for any significant length of time. Despite this, it is certain that it is an integral part of the history of Mineral County of which little has previously been written.

North and Beyond Chalk Hill

Following the road past past the chalk hill and Aldrich Station, it continues northerly toward and into what J. Ross Browne called the "Walker River Valley." Westerly from the road and off the beaten path, surveyor John G. Booker identified what he called an "Old Stone Cabin" and "Old Barn."

The map produced by John G. Booker during his sectional survey of T8N R27E, showed the "Old Stone Cabin" and "Old Barn" as being within the southwest quarter of Section 27, near a land feature noted as "Point of Rocks." When the cabin and barn were first constructed is not known at this time.

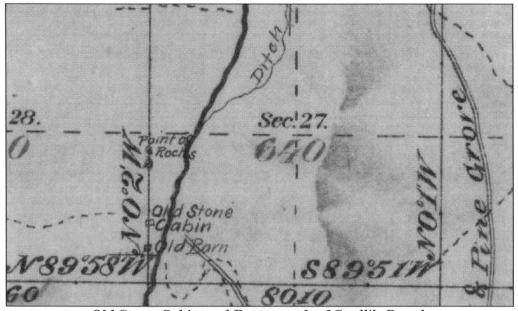

Old Stone Cabin and Barn, south of Grulli's Ranch
(General Land Office, T8N R27E, M. D. M.; John G. Booker, 1903)

In 1920, the family of John H. Glazier, who is known to have been involved in the establishment of Aurora's "Midway Resort" in the "Red-Light district" in 1915, was enumerated in the Wichman Precinct in Mineral County, just after the household of H. O. Lewis, who, by that time, had acquired land near the Grulli ranch. Living in the vicinity of the old stone cabin were Glazier's Indian wife, Sadie, and their two sons, Jimmie and Jack; his brother-in-law Bill Sam and mother-in-law, Mattie Sam. The household enumerated just after Glazier's family was that of "Joe Mathews," who was mentioned in the 1911 State Engineer's report as having succeeded to the water rights of A. Grulli.

In September, 1920, it was reported that, "Mr. Glazier brought a load of watermelons to Bridgeport from East Walker River district last Saturday and had little trouble in disposing of his entire load." (Bridgeport *Chronicle-Union*, 9/15/1920)

During the prohibition years of the 1920's, like so many other regular citizens Glazier ran afoul of the law while attempting to support his family. The incident was reported in the newspapers:

> "School Trustee Is Held By U.S. on Dry Charges.
> John H. Glazier, Mineral County rancher and school trustee, is in jail in Yerington facing a prohibition charge

following a raid conducted on his ranch on the east fork of the
Walker river yesterday, according to a report today of
prohibition enforcement officers upon their return to Reno. A
complete distilling outfit, fourteen gallons of moonshine
whiskey and 250 gallons of mash were discovered on the place."
(Reno Evening *Gazette*, 6/17/1924)

Glazier had endeavored to make contraband alcohol using honey,
as he lacked the money to purchase the sugar normally used in the
distilling process.

As a result of his arrest by the prohibition officers, Glazier may
have found it necessary to sell the home property where Sadie and the
children resided in the Wichman precinct along the East Walker River,
to two Yerington men in 1924.

The Glazier property was located within Section 27, in T8N R27E,
and included "one four room cabin, one one room cabin, one stable" and
other outbuildings. He did not, however, have a patent title to the land
on which his home was situated.

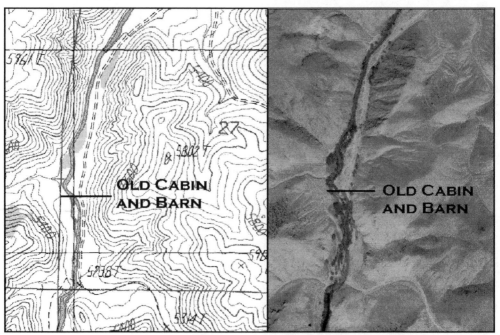

(USGS Mitchell Spring Quadrangle, Topo-1992 Aerial-2000)

In 1930, the Glazier family lived in Bridgeport Township, in Mono
County but, by 1938, they resided at Sweetwater, then in Lyon County,

Nevada. In that year, "Jack Glazier," as he was popularly known, was appointed as a School Trustee for the Sweetwater school. By 1940, the family had moved to Smith Valley, where they remained.

John H. Glazier, the last of those who had been associated with Aurora's "Red Light district," died in December, 1958, at the Reno Veterans' Hospital. He was buried at the Hillcrest Cemetery in Smith Valley, and was survived by his wife Sadie and his son James. Sons Jack and William had predeceased their father. Sadie Sam Glazier died four years later, in 1962, and is buried next to her husband.

East Walker River runs through numerous mountain canyons

Chapter 6

Grulli Ranch
Also part of Lewis Ranch
(Est. ca. 1895, in Section 22, T8N R27E, M.D.M)

The name of "A. Gruli" first appeared on the county tax assessment roll in 1894. The value of Gruli's property was listed at a mere $40. "Grullis House" was shown on the General Land Office map of T8N R27E, after John Booker's survey in 1901.

The State Engineer's report of 1911 noted the water rights of: "J. Mathews, Pine Grove, successor to A. Grulli: 67 acres, 1895, 1.07 second-feet; (from) Grulli ditches, East Walker." (Biennial Report of the State Engineer, 1909-1910, Appendix, Water Rights and Priorities as Established by the State Engineer, Walker River in Nevada, p. 151)

A native of Italy, farmer "Antone Gruli" [sic] was enumerated on the 1900 federal census at his ranch on the East Walker River. At 35 years of age, Mr. Grulli had been married for twelve years to his Italian-born wife, Minnie, who, with the couple's two children, Ida (age 6 years, born Nevada) and Manuel (age 5 years, born Nevada), lived with him on the ranch.

"Aniceto Gruli" acquired a land patent to his farm lands in Section 22, T8N R27E, from the government in June, 1905.

By 1907, "Joe Matthews" was assessed for the land and Grulli was not. In 1914, J. R. Mathews was assessed for property taxes for Grulli's Section 22 lands. According to an Abstract of Title, for the period of October 10, 1950 to January 23, 1951, Mathews had purchased the "North 12 acres of SW ¼ of NE ¼ [in Section 22, T8N, R27E]; said premises being the same lands conveyed August 20, 1913, by N. D. Lewis to J. R. Mathews, by deed recorded in Book 1 of Deeds, page 268, of Mineral County Records." (Washoe Title Insurance Company; copy of J. J. Connelly; on file at Mineral County Museum)

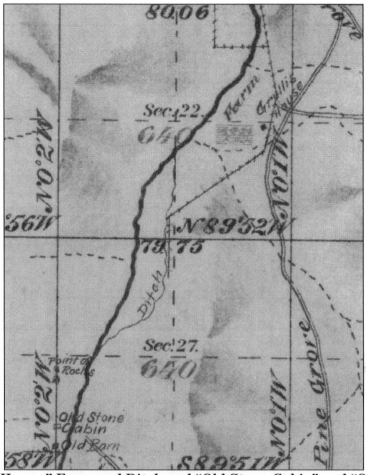

"Grullis House," Farm and Ditch and "Old Stone Cabin" and "Old Barn"
(General Land Office, T8N R27E, M.D.M., 10/17/1903)

By 1910, the Grulli family was residing in the Spragg Precinct, in Lyon County, per the census of that year. In 1920, Antone, Mary and Manuel were residing in the East Mason Valley Precinct, where they appear to have been living in the vicinity of other Italian immigrant families. Their daughter, Ida, had married Lawrence Masini, a resident of Yerington and vicinity. Ida Masini died in August, 1927 from the effects of an ulcer, and was buried at St. Joseph's Catholic Cemetery, in Yerington.

Sometime after February, 1911, the Bridgeport *Chronicle-Union* reported:

> "A Carson company with F. B. Whitelaw as superintendent, is arranging to do considerable work on the coal property near the Joe Mathews place on the East Walker and a short distance from the Aldrich cabin on the Bodie road [Aldrich Grade]. This company is putting on a boring machine which has a capacity of sinking to a depth of 600 or 700 feet, and proposes to give the ground a thorough test for coal, an inferior quality of which crops on the surface and shows to a slight depth." (Bridgeport *Chronicle-Union*, nd.; has notice dating to 2/21/1911)

Grulli Ranch, East Walker River
(USGS Aerial – Mitchell Spring Quadrangle, 8/2000)

Joe Mathews was enumerated in the 1900 census as Jose C. Mathews, living in the Mason Valley election precinct. A native of Portugal, he was a farmer and had been married for four years. His household included his Portuguese-born wife, Maria, and their three Nevada-born children, Annie, Alfred and Joseph, ages 3 years, 2 years and 9 months old, respectively. Jose had arrived in the United States in 1880 and Maria came in 1893. Antone Mathews, probably his brother, was enumerated in the dwelling before Jose's household.

The family of Joseph and Mary "Matthews" was listed on the 1910 federal census in the Spragg election precinct, Lyon County. The Joseph C. "Mathews" family was again enumerated in the Spragg precinct in 1920. In 1930, Jose and Maria Mathews were still in the Spragg precinct, with several of their children, including married daughter, Annie, the wife of Portuguese-born Joe Costello.

Joe Mathews, a native of the Azores Islands, died in April, 1933, at the age of 72 years. He had come to America when he was sixteen years old and "had been a resident of Mason Valley and the East Walker district for nearly forty years." He was survived by his son William, a granddaughter, Mrs. Frances Kennedy and a niece, Mrs. George, who resided in Merced, California. (Reno Evening *Gazette*, 4/25/1933) Mr. Mathews was buried in the Catholic cemetery at Yerington.

Joseph R. Matthews held the Grulli ranch property until 1929, after which time the 1930 tax assessment was made to P. G. (Perry G.) Morgan for the "Mathew's Ranch." In 1933, this area of Mineral County was segregated to Lyon County.

Settling on nearby lands was Harry O. Lewis, son-in-law of George A. Green of the Nine Mile Ranch. A native of Montana, Harry Lewis married Annetta Green around 1905. In 1910, the couple and their two children were enumerated near the ranch of Henry Morgan, in the Cambridge precinct of Mineral County.

Lewis was first assessed for the land in 1917. He was registered for the military draft in September of 1918. At that time his residence was at Wichman, Nevada. He reported that his nearest relative was Milton Lewis, living at Kelseyville, California.

In 1919, a unique find occurred on the Lewis ranch:

> "Imense [sic] Tooth Found in Ground.
> *Special to the Gazette* – Yerington, Oct. 13.
>
> During the excavations in the coal land on the Harry Lewis ranch on the East Walker, a large tooth was found. The ivory is of the grinder variety, measuring on the upper surface about three inches wide and seven inches long. There is a large deposit of lignite on the ranch which has been investigated only in a superficial manner until the present locators undertook to explore for oil.

In addition to the tooth there were many other bones, large and small but generally proportionate in size so that there is little doubt of their being the remains of a prehistoric monster. The tooth is well preserved, showing a thick, well worn enamel on the grinding surface, the mark of the line to which the gum extended and well defined traces of the rood set in the bony structure of the jaw. E. J. Ross is the finder." (Reno Evening *Gazette*, 10/13/1919)

In the early 1930's, former Nevada Governor, James G. Scrugham, wrote a column for the Nevada State *Journal*. In one column, Scrugham wrote of the area where H. O. Lewis' ranch was:

"Many gold and silver ore discoveries, including the one at Tonopah, have been attributed to acts of stray burros kicking off pieces of ledge matter. It remained for a deer to be responsible for the discovery of a large deposit of sub-bitumenous coal in Mineral county, in a wash adjacent to the East Walker river near Wichman.

Many years ago, Harry Lewis, a rancher in the district, was pursuing a buck deer through a heavy fall of snow. Going over a hillock, Lewis noticed that a sooty material resembling coal dust had been kicked out on the snow by the fleeing animal.

Returning to the spot after the snow had melted, Lewis found the outcroppings of a rotted coal seam, which ran high in heat values in spite of its disintegration.

Since that time, Mr. Lewis has run several thousand feet of exploratory work on the coal seams and has now developed some high grade beds of soft coal, averaging from six to ten feet in thickness. Tests are in progress to ascertain its heating value and mining costs, with a view of putting the fuel on the market during the coming winter.

In addition to the coal measures, the valley of the East Walker river contains numerous fossil beds, and some placer gold operations are now under way at the Ira Fallon place, formerly known as the Webster ranch. It is claimed that teeth and bones of long extinct monsters, like the mammoth and dinosaur are frequently found in the vicinity. Mr. Lewis has a number of such pieces in his possession, which bears out the contention that the East Walker valley once produced dense vegetation and was the home of numerous forms of animal life which have now become extinct, including the giant groundsloth [sic] and the saber toothed tiger." (Nevada State *Journal*, 7/26/1932)

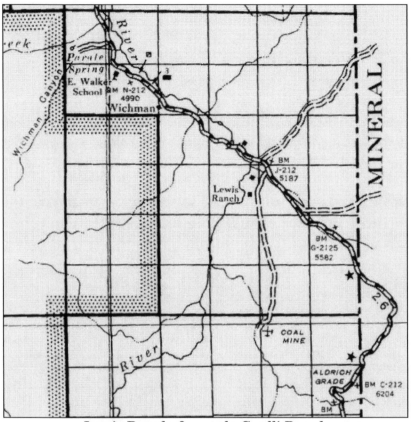

Lewis Ranch, formerly Grulli Ranch
(Nevada Dept. of Transportation Quad Map 2, 1953)

Harrison Oliver Lewis died in January, 1963 in Reno. Of his life in Nevada, in part, the Reno Evening *Gazette* reported:

"Mr. Lewis was born March 5, 1879, in Helena, Mont., to the late Milton and Sara B. Lewis. He moved to Mason Valley in 1884 and spent his youth in the Sweetwater area. He later moved to Nine Mile Ranch, where he operated an early-day cyanide plant.

At Nine Mile, Mr. Lewis met and married Annetta Green, daughter of a pioneer Nevada family, in 1904.

He engaged in mining and ranching on the East Walker River until his retirement in 1947. Mr. Lewis remained active in mining until he became ill." (Reno Evening *Gazette*, 1/28/1963)

In *The Valleys of the Walker Rivers* (Matheus, 1995), the author wrote about this ranch as follows:

> "Harry Lewis settled in this area. His land had a coal deposit which was used by the family. It is believed that a substantial oil deposit is on the land but the family has always been averse to the exploration of the area." (*The Valleys of the Walker Rivers*; Phyllis Matheus, 1995, p. 65)

In 1951, a party named McLaughlin was named as the owner or operator of the old Grulli and Lewis ranch lands. From 1952 to 1953, the name of Padias is noted in connection with the ranch. (Walker River Basin Irrigation Diversions, Summary of Historic Surface Water Irrigation Diversions; Appendix B., Table B-7, p. 4; Randy Pahl, P.E., 2000)

Today, the area of Grulli's ranch is shown to be a part of the Flying M Ranch, in a part of the East Walker River Scenic Area.

Chapter 7

Washington

Also known as the Cumberland Coal Mining District (1862),
Washington Mining District (1867) and Coal Valley (1879)
(Est. ca. 1862, in T8N R28E, M.D.M.)

This place is shown on several early maps, its location being
northeasterly from the Elbow Ranch. Little information is known of
the early years; however, several small news items help to add
knowledge of it, including this little notation in 1862:

> "Another Coal Discovery. – Cannel coal of an excellent
> quality has been recently discovered near Walker's river in the
> Esmeralda District. It is said to burn freely without much
> smell or smoke. The supply is said to be inexhaustible."
> (Sacramento Daily *Union*, 6/14/1862)

Later in June the San Francisco *Bulletin* wrote "Further of the
Coal Discovery in Esmeralda":

> "If we are to believe certain stories the Eastern slope will
> hereafter suffer no more want of fuel, as coal discoveries in
> various districts are being reported almost every day. The
> Esmeralda (Aurora) Star thus mentions one of the latest:
> A party of four men, consisting of Col. Mormon [sic], H. W.
> Johnson, Mr. Riley and William Given, started from Walker
> river for Aurora, and on their way on the first day of June,
> immediately after leaving the last crossing coming this way,

some of the party proposed to leave the trail and turn to the left and hunt antelope, which was agreed to. After having left the trail and separating, traveling about a mile and a half, one of the party (Given) had his attention attracted to a singular looking substance which resembled old rotton [sic] tobacco. He stooped and examined it, and finding it to be hard like rock ascended an eminence near at hand and saw Col. Mormon. He called him to come and see it, who came, and knocking off some of the surface fragments, found that it was coal. They brought some of it to town, and trying it at a blacksmith's forge, proved it to be coal of the very best quality by welding several pieces of iron together very satisfactorily. The district in which this coal is found extends about a mile and a half wide and two miles long, and is not more than 18 miles from Aurora, to which a good wagon road can be made at an expense not to exceed $1,500. It is on a direct line to Fort Churchill and Virginia, and a good road at all seasons of the year, and easy grade can be had.

On the 4th June, the district was organized under the name of the "Cumberland Coal Mining District." Col. Mormon was chosen Chairman of the meeting, and W. S. Yager appointed Secretary. A rule was adopted limiting each claim to 500 feet on the bed or vein, including all the spurs or strata branching out to the distance of 100 feet. Peter Ingram was elected Recorder of the district. We are indebted to Father Yager for the above information, and he also says that the supply will be unlimited and the coal will compare favorably with that of the Cumberland mountains in East Tennessee." (San Francisco *Bulletin*, 6/24/1862)

The *California Farmer and Journal of Useful Sciences* reprinted an article from the *Esmeralda Star* newspaper in Aurora, the editor of which had personally visited the area of the coal discoveries:

"The Coal Mines of the Eastern Slope.
The Editor of the Esmeralda Star has recently visited these mines. He says: We left Aurora in the morning, and on arriving at the Five Mile Ranch remained there about two hours waiting for Col. Moorman, one of the original discoverers of the mines.

From thence we rode on to the Nine Mile Ranch, owned by Mr. Gardner. From this place we pushed on for about seven miles over a sage-brush country towards a gap in the mountains, and reached the rim of a basin about a mile in diameter and about four hundred feet in depth. The bottom of this basin is broken up into small hills and are nearly as white as chalk. On its northern side are high hills of the same character; descending the slope on the south side and passing over these small hills, we found them to be like ash heaps, our horses sinking in over their fetlocks. This substance on examination proved to be burnt or bleached clay and in small flakes or shales. This basin is totally destitute of either water or soil. On leaving the bottom and ascending a gradual slope of this same white shalestone or tabular spar, on the northeastern side we came to a small pine bush and fount two notices reading: "This is to certify that I the undersigned A. B., claim one-half mile due north, thence due east one-half mile, thence due south one-half mile, thence to the place of the beginning and that I have taken it up for coal mining and agricultural purposes."

This last *agricultural purposes* took us down. The man that put up those notices must have been engaged in horticultural and pomological pursuits in endeavoring to raise strawberries and peaches in an immense lime kiln that had been well burnt.

Passing out of this basin and continuing on about a mile further, we gradually descended a broken country until we arrived at Sulphur Springs, where there is good water, and here we made preparations to encamp for the night...

We arose at an early hour in the morning, got through breakfast by sunrise and pushed on down to the coal beds. A mile down the ravine which leads from the spring, we came to a well defined strata of bituminous coal, which is three feet wide, and dipping at an angle of forty-five degrees and continuing an indefinite distance. The coal from this vein is of a very superior quality and burns readily.

Continuing along down, strata after strata continued to present itself and were as easy to be traced as streaks of charcoal across mounds of chalk. The most deserving of mention are the "Cumberland," "Ben Franklin," "Mammoth," "Black Diamond," and "Land Slide;" all of them handsomely defined ledges or veins cropping out and running thousands of feet. The croppings resemble a lot of rotten hemlock or pine bark laid regularly along the cord wood and then tipped over and standing on end at an angle of forty-five degrees.

The "Black Diamond" pitches more up hill than the others and crops out on the other side of a high chalky cliff and can be seen for several miles.

The "Mammoth" lies more flat but is not quite so wide as the "Black Diamond," but is equally as good a ledge.

The "Cumberland," out of which we took four sacks of as good coal as ever was seen, we think is the best, judging from its appearance, and the abundance of bituminous shale mixed with silex, alumine and lime found upon the surface. Some of the fragments which we picked up were nearly as large as our hand and transparent as glass.

There is a large basin about ten miles in diameter, nearly surrounded by the mountains, with large gaps between them left by nature for either wagon or railroads. All of these veins of coal dip towards the center of this basin, in which are large flats or slightly inclined planes, where we think the great mass of coal is deposited.

The distance from Aurora to these mines is about twenty-one miles; to Sulphur Springs, eighteen. The distance to Walker river from the mines is about six miles further. A good road can be built for $1000 or $1200 to the Carson road, intersecting it at Gardner's Ranch, from thence it is a good road all the way to this place and we are informed a good road can be made to Dayton and Fort Churchill from these mines, which are on a direct air line from Aurora to those localities.

In order to develop these mines there should be an incorporated company to each vein, and but few in a company at that. We learn that a proposition has been made to consolidate the interests of the entire coal region; such a course is not feasible, and entirely impracticable. There are hundreds of claims and notices put up where there is nothing but a slight grayish discoloration of ashy surface which amount to nothing; and the entire interests of the mining of gold and silver of Esmeralda might, with a better show of reasoning, be consolidated, than those of the Coal District.

We have thus given a full, and we think a fair description of these coal mines, and as yet do not own the interest of a single foot in them, but we intend to, if we can be so fortunate. It is only a question of time, and very short at that, when they will be estimated and held at their proper value." (*California Farmer and Journal of Useful Sciences*, Vol. 17, Number 18, 7/25/1862)

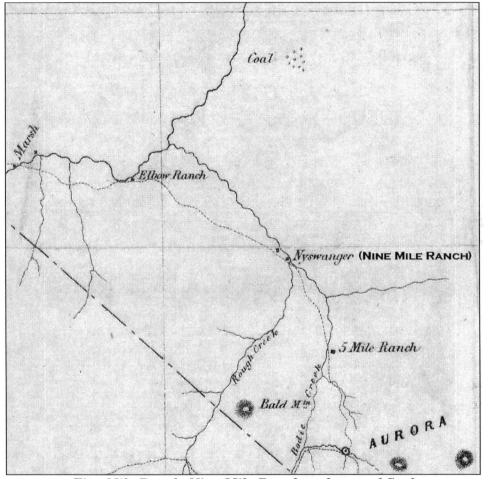

Five Mile Ranch, Nine Mile Ranch and area of Coal
(Map of the Public Surveys in Nevada Territory; General Land Office, October 1862)

Perhaps in a move to build the road suggested by Edwin A. Sherman, the *Star's* editor, John W. Pugh, councilmember to the Nevada Territorial Legislature from Esmeralda, gave "notice of a toll road franchise bill in favor of L. Wilbourn and R. Lyons, for a toll road on East Walker river, near Dixon's ranch, Esmeralda." (Sacramento Daily *Union*, 11/22/1862) Pugh introduced the bill for a "toll bridge franchise for Lyons and Welburn's bridge across Walker River," on November 22nd, 1862. (Sacramento Daily *Union*, 11/25/1862) The quartz mill of "Welburn &

Van Horn" on the East Walker River was reported in 1861 to be approximately 26 miles downstream from the Elbow Ranch. (Sacramento Daily *Union*, 12/12/1861) "Wilburn's arrastras, driven by water on the East Walker, 30 miles north of Aurora," was reported to have been doing well before the flood in the January, 1862. (San Francisco *Bulletin*, 2/1/1862). The toll road and toll bridge were likely to accommodate access to the mills.

"Doctor," a correspondent of the Daily *Alta California*, in early March, 1862 wrote about "Mining Matters" in and about Aurora and its vicinity. He wrote that some locations on "Walker river" had revealed silver deposits and that "Coal is also to be found there." (Daily *Alta California*, 3/12/1863) Another correspondent, possibly Samuel Youngs, wrote later in March about minerals and specimens sent to the General Land Office, in Washington, D. C., which included "rich gold and silver rock; ...coal found in large quantities near the east branch of the Walker river," and other minerals that had been located in the area. (Sacramento Daily *Union*, 3/21/1863)

In a letter from Aurora, dated March 31, 1867, a correspondent wrote the Sacramento Daily *Union*, that:

> "The most favorable reports continue to be brought in from Pine Grove and Washington Districts, near Walker river – the latter particularly – as the ledges are large, being from five to thirty feet wide, well defined, with perfect casings. The rock is silver bearing, with a percentage of copper. The last cleanup of Captain Cheever's mill netted $66 to the ton. He is building a furnace to test and work the rock in Washington District. Plenty of wood and water power are in the immediate vicinity of the mines." (Sacramento Daily *Union*, 4/6/1867, Matters in Aurora, Nev.)

Almost a month later, in April, a correspondent advised that at the "Washington District the ledges are being developed, and the people have great confidence in their richness." (Sacramento Daily *Union*, 4/27/1867, Matters in Aurora, Nev.) In support of the *Union's* correspondent, a writer to the Daily *Alta California* also wrote:

> "The Esmeralda *Union*, speaking of the same section, says:
> The lately discovered district of Washington, near Pine Grove,

on Walker River, is attracting the attention of capitalists, and from information from what we consider reliable sources and from assays made of the ore, we have but little doubt as to the extent, richness and permanence of the mines of this district. A town has been laid out at the mines and christened Washington. There is plenty of wood and water in the immediate vicinity of the mines. Buildings are being erected, the mines are being worked, and the most encouraging feature of the camp is, that the present owners are not on the sell." (Daily *Alta California*, 4/29/1867, quoting *Territorial Enterprise*.)

Washington District, area of Elbow Ranch
(Map of California and Nevada; Holt, 1869)

An additional report was made on the Washington District in early September, which noted that "very favorable reports" continued to come in from there. It also informed that:

> "Brooks will have his eight stamp mill there in about four weeks, after which we shall hear something more definite from the district." (Sacramento Daily *Union*, 9/5/1867)

The following month, in October, 1867 another letter arrived at the Sacramento Daily *Union's* offices, in which the writer advised:

> "I saw a very pretty specimen of ruby silver, brought from the Eclipse ledge, in Washington District, last week, and am

informed the rock is steadily improving in richness as the ledge is opened...Brooks' mill has commenced crushing; but I am informed he will not work first-class at present, or until he has put up roasting furnaces. (Sacramento Daily *Union*, 10/11/1867)

In an article in the Sacramento Daily *Union* of November 14, 1867, the paper wrote of "Coal, Copper, etc.":

"We were shown yesterday by W. Troop, a resident of Yolo county, but recently from Nevada, a sample of coal discovered by him in the northern part of Esmeralda county. He and his associates had sunk an incline seventy feet into the hill, and the sample shown us was taken from that depth. The vein at that point was four feet thick.

The coal has been tested in a blacksmith's forge and for culinary purposes, and is found to burn freely. The experiment of distilling oil from this coal has also been tried with success. The location of the mine is about fifty miles south of the Pacific Railroad.

Troop also exhibits rich specimens of copper ore taken from a lode six feet thick, located two miles north of the coal mine. He also has in his possession specimens of silver ore taken from a lode in the Washington District. This lode is nine feet thick at a depth of seventeen feet. Several tons worked at a mill at Franktown yielded about $240 per ton."

In a letter to the Sacramento Daily *Union* from an Aurora correspondent, dated December 31, 1867, the writer reported a recent storm had caused flooding and that from "East Walker I hear that Brooks mill at Washington is safe." (Sacramento Daily *Union*, 1/11/1868)

In June, 1868, a writer from Aurora wrote that: "I am informed that Brooks, who put a mill in Washington district last year, found the rock, which is silver-bearing and has a large percentage of galena of that refractory character that he could not work it satisfactorily by the ordinary mill process, has now made arrangements with a party at Carson to put up smelting works, so that he can work the rock, which is said to be rich, and abundance of it, effectually, and the district assume the prosperous   position which has been expected and it is justly entitled to." (Sacramento Daily *Union*, 6/5/1868)

A correspondent from Aurora to the Sacramento Daily *Union*, in May, 1873, noted:

> "A man came in here yesterday and informs me that he is working a coal mine about eighteen miles from here, and this side of Walker River. They are now down about sixty feet in the mine, and the water is now troubling them, although they are yet a thousand feet above the river. He says the ledge is about six feet wide and growing wider as they go down. The coal is a very good quality and burns freely. They use it for cooking and their fires generally. He says they have sent samples to Carson and had very favorable reports of it. He feels fully confident of success, and says there are other mines in the vicinity which he has taken up." (Sacramento Daily *Union*, 5/22/1873)

In April of 1879, the U. S. Postmaster established a post office at Washington, Esmeralda County, appointed John M. Coleman as postmaster on the 16th of the month. A little over a year later, in July of 1880, the Washington Post Office was discontinued. The Washington post office may have been the only post office established along the East Walker River, beyond the short lived Elbow Ranch post office in the 1880's.

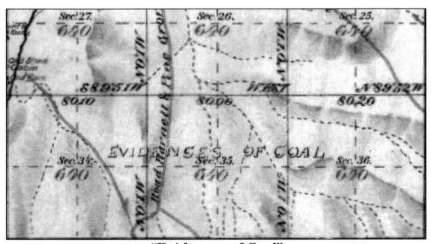

"Evidences of Coal"
(General Land Office, T8N R27E, M. D. M., John G. Booker, 1903)

In his 1903 survey field notes of T8N R27E, John G. Booker discussed this area in his notes of its General Description:

"In the southeastern portion the formation is sand stone, to a great extent, and a poor quality of coal has been found in section 36.

Sections 27-28-33 and 34 possess evidence of mineral and of an abandoned mining District, Known as Washington District."

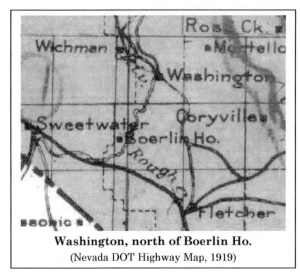

Washington, north of Boerlin Ho.
(Nevada DOT Highway Map, 1919)

Interestingly, the town of Washington was shown on the Nevada Department of Transportation's map of the State's highways, even though the town had for decades been defunct.

In the 1920's several federal land patents were issued for "Coal Lands." George Brodigan, once the Nevada Secretary of State, patented the East half of the East half of Section 35, T8N R27E and Leslie L. A. Green, son of Nine Mile Ranch owner, George S. Green, patented the West half of the West half of Section 35, T8N R27E.

Around the same time, in two separate patents, Harry Lewis and his wife, Annetta Lewis received Coal Land patents for portions of Section 36, T8N R27E and Section 1 of T7N R27E, the latter land being just west of Aldrich Station.

In October, 1920 Mono National Forest Supervisor William M. Maule noted in his daily diary that he had visited several of the ranches on the "E. side." On the night of the 20th, he stayed overnight at the Morgan Ranch and on the 21st, he wrote:

> "Rode up to Coal valley and went through the new operations of coal prospects. Good ledges of low grade coal. They are burning it in hoist boilers and seem to make steam quite well. They have sale for it in Bodie but no delivery yet. Returned to Sweetwater via Fletchers and Elbow." (William M. Maule, "Diaries Of William M. Maule, Forest Supervisor, Mono National Forest (Nevada & California) 1909-1938" TMs [photocopy], transcribed by Wynne M. Maule, Bridgeport Office, Humboldt-Toiyabe National Forest, USDA Forest Service)

From early maps reviewed, it is suspected that the location of the town of Washington, if it ever did actually become a town, was in the vicinity of what later became Grulli's ranch, though Washington was clearly shown on the west side of the East Walker River. The following map views show the comparison of the location of Washington and Grulli's ranch.

Sites of
Washington 1873 (L) and Grulli's House 1903 (R)
at bend in East Walker River

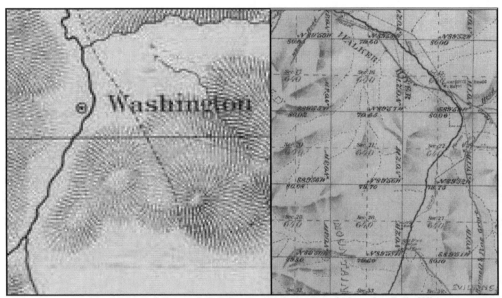

(L) – Topographical Map of Central California, with a part of Nevada; J. D. Whitney, 1873
(R) – General Land Office, Sec. 22, T8N R27E, M. D. M., Booker, 1903

Background Note:
The earliest year's of the State saw the emergence of thousands of mining districts, like Washington Mining District, that were formed at the first discoveries found in the area. Some of the districts survived, many being known still today. Like the Washington Mining District, some died and were never heard of again. Others would be replaced by later districts that were formed under different names.

Chapter 8

Morgan Ranch

(Est. ca. 1879, in Section 15, T8N R27E, M.D.M.)

The 1911 State Engineer's report of water rights on the East Walker River included: "H. S. Morgan: 58 acres, 1879, .93 second-feet; 10 acres, 1889, .16 second-feet; 92 acres, 1894, 1.46 second-feet; (from) Morgan's ditches on East Fork." (Biennial Report of the State Engineer, 1909-1910, Appendix, Water Rights and Priorities as Established by the State Engineer, Walker River in Nevada, p. 151)

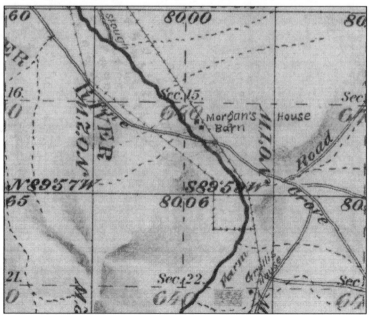

Morgan's House and Barn, north of Grulli's Ranch
(General Land Office Map, T8N R27E, M.D.M., 10/17/1903)

In J. Ross Browne's 1865 article in *Harper's New Monthly Magazine* about "The Walker River Country," Browne wrote:

> "A few farms had been started on the bottom lands, and we passed some very cozy little farmhouses and thrifty gardens. The river is fringed with willow, sycamore, and a species of cotton-wood, resembling balm of Gilead. We followed its course about seven miles through a series of narrow valleys, on the left side, till we reached a gorge in the mountains through which it passes. At this point there is a good ford, over which we crossed. Lawson's Ranch commences here. A drive of half a mile took us to the house; a frame shanty pleasantly situated near the road. Mr. Lawson was at home, and kindly offered us the accommodations of his place...
>
> Lawson's Ranch may be considered the beginning of the main East Walker River Valley. The bottom gradually widens. On the right lies a sloping plain, barren in appearance but abounding in some of the finest lands east of the Sierras. A survey of this country has recently been made by Major E. A. Sherman, under the auspices of a company of Aurorians, with a view of opening it up for settlement. It is in contemplation to make a canal or acequia from Lawson's Ford for the purpose of irrigating the extensive tract of land now lying waste between the foot-hills and the river bottom..." (J. Ross Browne, *Harper's New Monthly Magazine*, Vol. 31, Issue 186, November 1865)

Browne's description of Lawson's Ranch, while not verified as such, may have been at or near the same location where the Morgan Ranch was later established. Especially telling is that a ford was associated with the Lawson Ranch and Morgan Ranch was associated with the first bridge crossing on the Aurora to Pine Grove road.

The first county tax assessment naming H. S. Morgan came in the year 1886, for a valuation of $430. By 1891, Morgan's property had an assessed value of $2,630. Morgan obtained a federal land patent to portions of Section 15, T8N R27E, in November of 1905.

Henry S. Morgan was born "on the Plains," in or around October, 1852, and was the son of William H. and Ruth Morgan, natives of Kentucky and Illinois, respectively. In the 1860 and again in the 1870 census, the Morgan family resided in Lane County, Oregon; at Eugene in the latter year. Henry's place of birth changed to Oregon on the 1870 census.

In mid-December 1879, Morgan was married to Maine native, Mina E. (Amina Elizabeth) Fish, the daughter of Amos Fish and the sister of Amos Fish, Jr. (Esmeralda County Marriages, Vol. A, p. 371)

In 1880, Mr. and Mrs. Morgan resided at Pine Grove, where Amina's brother, Amos Fish, boarded with them. In this year, Morgan was working as a teamster. In the residence enumerated previous to the Morgan household, lived Mrs. Morgan's sister, Amanda J. Moses, wife of quartz miner Othniel (Otho) Moses. The latter and his father, millwright P. P. (Philo Plinney) Moses were enumerated at Pine Grove on the 1875 Nevada State Census. Amos Fish Jr. committed suicide at Pine Grove in early October, 1892. He was buried at Carson City and rests in an unmarked grave.

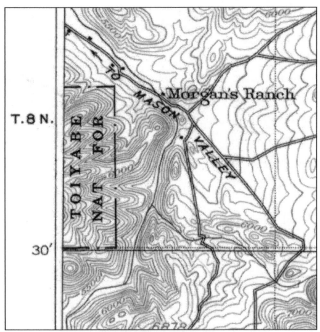

Morgan's Ranch
(USGS Hawthorne Quadrangle, 1909)

By 1900, Henry Morgan's family had filled out nicely, including sons Perry G. (19 years) and William H. (17 years), and daughters Clara A. (15 years) and Hattie L. (14 years). In this year the family was enumerated on the census north of Aniceto Grulli's ranch in the Cambridge Precinct, near the location of Morgan's ranch. They remained on the ranch to the census of 1910. In this year, son Perry was driving freight in the new mining camp of Lucky Boy, south of Hawthorne.

At 67 years of age, Henry Morgan stayed on the ranch, which was enumerated in the Wichman Precinct on the 1920 Census. The Morgan ranch household was counted between the households of H. O. Lewis and John Wichman.

Mrs. Morgan died in June, 1930, at the age of 74 years. Henry S. Morgan died at the home of his daughter, Mrs. Henry Boerlin, on February 26, 1933. Two differing accounts of his life in Nevada were published at the time of his death. The first was from Hawthorne, in which was written:

> "H. S. Morgan, one of the real pioneers of Mineral county, died Sunday night at the home of his daughter, Mrs. Henry Boerlin.
> Morgan came to Mineral county in 1874 and had lived here ever since as a miner and rancher. He made the Morgan ranch famous for its hospitality..." (Nevada State *Journal*, 3/3/1933, datelined Hawthorne, March 2)

The other article appeared in the Reno Evening *Gazette* of March 4th, and included:

> "...When nineteen years of age he arrived in Carson valley where he remained for a short time before moving to Mason valley where he resided at Pine Grove. On December 11, 1879, he married Mina Elizabeth Fish and moved to Glenbrook where he engaged in logging for a number of years. He returned to Pine Grove during the early days of its gold rush and leased until 1888, when he purchased a ranch on the East Walker. He resided on the ranch until the death of his wife on May 29, 1930. Following his wife's death he made his home with his daughter, Mrs. L. W. Osborne, of Yerington."

The Morgan family members are buried in the Valley View Cemetery, in Yerington, where most of the graves are marked. Clara Morgan Boerlin McInnis and her two husbands, Henry Boerlin (Jr.) and Guy A. McInnis, rest in the cemetery at Hawthorne. Clara and Henry's graves are unmarked.

In 1939, news of the sale of four of the East Walker River ranches was reported:

"Max Fleischmann Buys Ranch Holdings

Purchase of four cattle ranches in the East Walker river district by Major Max Fleischmann for $160,000 was announced today by Norman Biltz and associates, who handled the transaction.

The properties include the Ira Fallon, Morgan Brothers, Polly [sic] and Green [Nine Mile] ranch holdings, an area located about thirty-five miles south of Yerington. Edward McConnell, who formerly engaged in the livestock business in the eastern part of the state, has been named manager of the holdings, it was announced. He has resided at Madera, Calif., for the past three years.

The four ranches have a total area of about 7000 acres, 1500 acres of which are under cultivation, and are the base property for nearly 250,000 acres of public domain and range land rights. The ranches were purchased from the Morgan family and the California Lands Company." (Reno Evening *Gazette*, 8/3/1939)

East Walker River, looking north near the old Morgan Ranch

Born in 1877 in Riverside, Ohio, Maximilian Charles Fleischman was the son of Austrian-born Charles L. Fleischmann. His father and uncle immigrated to America around 1867 and began the company that was the first to commercially manufacture yeast for sale. When he was a boy his father taught him about the business, which, upon the death of Mr. Fleischman, he and his brother, Julius Fleischmann, would continue to operate.

Although much of his life was involved in the family's business, Max Fleischmann was an avid sportsman, be it baseball, boxing or big game hunting. In 1905, he was married to Sarah Hamilton Sherlock, the daughter of Mr. and Mrs. J. C. Sherlock, an associate of Fleischmann's. Together this dynamic couple travelled to the North Pole as part of their honeymoon plans. They later went hunting in Africa and elsewhere.

During World War I, Fleischmann served in the Balloon Service of the U. S. Army. at the rank of Major. Previously an avid balloon aviator, Fleischmann and his partner, A. Holland Forbes, had established the air speed record for a balloon in 1909. On his discharge from the Army, Fleischmann was a Lt. Colonel, but the moniker of "Major Fleischmann" was preferred by him.

After two years of separation during the Great War (World War I), Max Fleischmann found it necessary to go to the British Isles on business. Having been away from his wife for this extended period of time, he would not go if Sarah was not with him. This was stated on his passport application in 1919, accompanied by their photographs at the time.

Max C. and Sarah H. Fleischmann (1919)

Later, after residing in various California cities, in 1935 Max Fleischmann selected a lakeside parcel near Glenbrook, at Lake Tahoe, Nevada. Taxes in California were cited as one of the reasons that Fleischmann made his move to the Silver State, although he continued to maintain residential property at Montecito, near Santa Barbara.

At Glenbrook, Fleischmann built a 36 acre estate, the home of which was cited to have cost some $200,000 to $250,000 when completed in 1936. The estate was planned to include the two-story dwelling, a six car garage, a six room guest house and a caretaker's residence located at the driveway entrance to the property. Thus, one of America's richest men arrived in Nevada and later became one of the State's most benevolent philanthropists.

Max C. Fleischmann

At the age of 74 years, in 1951 Fleischmann was diagnosed with terminal pancreatic cancer discovered during an operation. On the night of October 16, 1951, Max C. Fleischmann dined with his physician and when alone in his room after dinner, he shot himself through the mouth and died. Close friends opined they believed he committed this act to save his wife of 46 years the agony of watching him as he wasted away.

On his death the Max C. Fleischmann Foundation was established, as directed by Fleischmann in his last will and testament. Only one million dollars of his estate was distributed to individuals, with the remainder of his wealth going to the foundation. At his direction, the Foundation was to provide grant funding to specific projects involving religious, educational, charitable and scientific nonprofit organizations in the United States.

Fleischmann planned that the foundation would not live in perpetuity and directed that the funds should be distributed no later than the 20th year after the death of his wife, Sarah. Mrs. Fleischmann died in early July, 1961, which set the clock ticking on the Foundation's trustees directive to distribute the remaining funds. Initially funded with approximately fifty million dollars, by the year the funds were to have been depleted, there was said to be some ninety-eight million dollars remaining in the Trustees' hands.

It took them a year longer than directed, but, by July 1982, all of the Max C. Fleischmann Foundation funds had been distributed to worthy organizations and causes. In Nevada alone, the Foundation funded many local and state projects, including a part of the funding for the Mineral County Museum and the Mineral County Library.

Now thirty-two years after the dissolution of the Max C. Fleischmann Foundation, evidence of Fleischmann's contributions to Nevada may be found on buildings and facilities throughout the State. Although many people today may not know his name, it is certain that Fleischmann's legacy and benevolence continues to live on.

The Nevada State *Journal* reported in 1945 that the "Fleischman [sic] Ranch" had been sold. The following particulars and history were provided:

> "Purchase by John V. Mueller of Reno of the Max C. Fleishman [sic] ranch and livestock holdings in Lyon and Mineral counties in Nevada and Mono county, California, was announced yesterday.
>
> Approximately 10,000 acres of land are included in the deal and embraced the Morgan, Webster, Wichman, Polli [sic], Green and Gregory ranches which were consolidated by Major Fleishman a few years ago. In the last five years Major Fleishman made many improvements including the erection of a very substantial home. Mueller said he expected to carry on the work and operate the property. Several thousand head of cattle were sold with the ranch.
>
> Several of the ranch units are associated with the early days of Aurora, Bodie and the East Walker river area. Three of the old stations used during the boom days of Bodie are intact.
> Major Fleishman is concentrating his ranch holdings in Jacks Valley, near Carson City where he acquired several thousand acres recently." (Nevada State *Journal*, 11/21/1945)

Mueller's ownership of the ranches is not identified in a Department of Conservation and Natural Resources report identifying the various owners of the ranches along the East Walker River. Instead, after Fleischmann's ownership, "East Walker Ranches," is the owner listed as owner. (Walker River Basin Irrigation Diversions, Summary of Historic Surface Water Irrigation Diversions; Appendix B., Table B-7, p. 4; Randy Pahl, P.E., 2000)

In an item titled, "Lyon Produces Big Hay Crop," it was reported that, "An unusually good yield of meadow hay and pasture forage on the Nine Mile unit of the ranch is reported by J. D. Crummer, owner of the property..." (Reno Evening *Gazette*, 11/21/1947) Three years later another article related to a law suit filed about an oil deal in Elko County, reported that Crummer had been "engaged in ranching in Lyon County and owned the East Walker Ranches until about two years ago..." (Nevada State *Journal*, 10/7/1950)

Contrary to what was written by the Nevada State *Journal*, above, the Reno Evening *Gazette* identified that "Mr. William Holmes, owner of the East Walker ranches," addressed a meeting in Yerington about a proposal for youth recreation center. (Reno Evening *Gazette*, 5/19/1949)

In September of 1950, the Reno Evening *Gazette* reported on the sale by Clayton E. Gunn of the Lucky Seven Ranch, a well known stock ranch at McDermitt, Humboldt County. Gunn also owned "the East Walker ranches at Yerington which he will continue to operate." (Reno Evening *Gazette*, 9/19/1950) Gunn was later killed in airplane crash near Oakland, California, in August 1951. (Reno Evening *Gazette*, 8/25/1951)

According to an Abstract of Title, for the period of October 10, 1950 to January 23, 1951, Clayton E. Gunn sold the East Walker Ranches to C. C. and Eileen E. Pierce in September 1950. The instrument of transfer conditioned the sale with: "Provided always, and this conveyance is made subject to a mortgage wherein Max C. Fleishmann is designated as mortgagee..."(Washoe Title Insurance Company; copy of J. J. Connelly; on file at Mineral County Museum) The Pierce's transferred the ranch properties to George Virgil Larson and his wife, Bernice, on November 1, 1950. The instrument of this transfer noted that the "deed is also subject to a certain mortgage dated January 15, 1949, executed by William D Holmes and Mary K. Holmes, his wife, to secure an indebtedness of $100,000...Dated January 14, 1949, in favor of Max C. Fleischmann..." (Washoe Title Insurance Company; J. J. Connelly)

In 1953, the area of the Morgan and Grulli ranches was shown on a Nevada Department of Transportation map to be the "Lewis Ranch." Lewis was the son-in-law of George A. Green, of the Nine Mile Ranch.

In 1954, the East Walker River ranches changed hands once more:

"East Walker Ranch Purchase Is Announced.

Sale of the East Walker ranches on the East Walker river 23 miles south of Yerington was announced today by Hamilton McCaughey, who handled the transaction for Ben Edwards and Associates of Reno.

A. Stanley [sic] Murphy of San Francisco purchased the property from Harold Hadley of San Diego for an undisclosed purchase price which McCaughey placed as close to a quarter of a million dollars.

The spread is made up of seven old ranches including six located along a 12 mile stretch of the East Walker, in addition to the famous Nine Mile ranch in a high mountain meadow about nine miles to the south. The property contains nearly 4000 acres of deed land, and a large portion of which is under irrigation in alfalfa and pasture.

Deeded land controls an area of federal range about 30 miles long and several miles wide containing an additional 150,000 acres. The ranch is said to have some of the best water rights out of the East Walker river and Bodie and Rough creeks, plus a valuable right to more than 3300 acre feet of stored water in the Bridgeport reservoir. More than 1000 head of cattle can be carried on the overall operation.

Located along the route of the old stage coaches, the [Nine Mile] ranch has a historic background. Some of the old hand-hewn stone buildings, like the hotel and livery stable, still stand. It is said that a large horde of gold coins and nuggets was buried near the present headquarters during the 1880's and there is no record they were ever recovered.

The late Maj. Max Fleischmann with the help of Paddy Doyle put the present ranch together in the early 1940's. He improved the ranch extensively, rehabilitating all the old buildings, installing 75 miles of fencing, putting in air strips and making it one of the outstanding commercial "show" ranches in Nevada.

Mr. Murphy is the president of Pacific Lumber Co. regarded as the largest redwood lumber operation in the world with extensive operations in California. He also has other ranch holdings in California and now resides principally in San

Francisco but with Mrs. Murphy plans to become a resident of Nevada and eventually retire to the ranch.

He and Mrs. Murphy are widely known as sportsmen. His immediate plans call for an intensive development, improvement and stocking program, to run both a commercial herd of Herefords and the famous Santa Gertrudis cattle."
(Reno Evening *Gazette*, 9/21/1954)

When Robert Harold Hadley acquired the ranches is not as yet known, but he may have purchased it from Harry Jackson (Jack) Crummer. In 1956, textile industry executive and San Diego native, Robert Harold Hadley, Sr., purchased the Flat Creek Ranch, in Humboldt County, Nevada. A year later he sold the Flat Creek Ranch and, shortly after, Hadley and his son, Robert Harold Hadley, Jr., purchased the historic Horseshoe Ranch, in Elko County. They sold the Horseshoe Ranch in 1958, retaining another ranch on Maggie Creek, which was operated under the corporation of the Hadley Ranches.

Robert Harold Hadley, Sr. died in 1962. Son, Bob Hadley, eventually settled at Sundance, Crook County, Wyoming, where the Hadley family owns the Sy Ranch, raising and selling live stock. Jim W. Hadley, son of Bob Hadley and grandson of Robert Harold Hadley, Sr., is presently a Commissioner of Crook County.

Albert Stanwood Murphy
President, Pacific Lumber Company

A. Stanwood Murphy was a native of Michigan, and the grandson of Simon J. Murphy, Sr., a lumberman from Maine. His father, Albert M. Murphy, was a native of Maine and a lumberman in Wisconsin during Stanwood Murphy's childhood. His father and others, acquired control of the Pacific Lumber Company, in Humboldt County, California in 1905. Mr. Murphy joined his father's vast redwood lumber business, eventually rising to become its president.

During the ownership and operation of the Pacific Lumber Company, A. S. Murphy instituted a sustained yield logging practice in order to ensure the redwood forests owned by the company would continue to develop later growths of redwood stands. It was a practice the family continued until the Murphy's lost control of the company in a hostile takeover in 1985.

Another report of the sale of the East Walker ranches was made in 1964:

> "$1.5 Million Sale?
> Couple Buys Flying-M Ranch
> *Special to The Journal*
>
> Yerington – Purchase of the Flying-M Ranch, located south of Yerington along the East Walker River, has been made by Mr. and Mrs. Stewart Abercrombie of Ranch Tiajguas, Santa Barbara. Former owners are Stanwood A. and June D. Murphy of San Francisco.
>
> Exact price of the more than 440,000 acre ranch was not disclosed but it reportedly was in the neighborhood of $1,500,000.
>
> Hamilton McCaughey of Reno, ranch investment counselor, handled the sale. Escrow covering the transaction is expected to close by April 1, 1965.
>
> The ranch is composed of eight old ranch units along 17 miles of the East Walker River, plus scattered deeded acreages in the Bodie Hills area. Summer headquarters is the extensive Nine Mile meadows.
>
> The range supports more than 2,500 head of cattle year around.
>
> The late A. S. Murphy introduced crossbred Santa Gertrudis cattle to the ranch, and today the herd is one of the largest outside the state of Texas." (Nevada State *Journal*, 12/7/1964)

The sale reported above was made by A. S. Murphy's son, Stanwood Albert Murphy and his surviving widow, the former June Dibble.

In 1968, the ranches of Morgan and Grulli were shown to be part of the Flying M Ranch. The Flying M Ranch continues in ownership of these early day ranches.

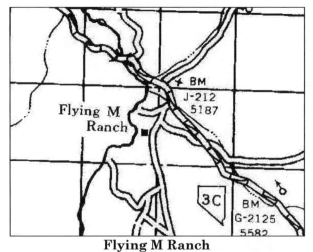

Flying M Ranch
(Nevada Department of Transportation Quadrangle Map No. 2, 1968)

Morgan & Grulli Ranches, now part of Flying M Ranch
(USGS Aerial – Mitchell Spring Quadrangle, 8/2000)

Chapter 9

Wright Ranch
Also known as Buckley's House and Wichman Ranch
(Est. ca. 1879, in Section 9, T8N R27E, M.D.M.)

A little northwest of the Morgan Ranch, James H. Wright was assessed for property valued at $1,835 in the year 1883, and for each subsequent year through 1901. The Pennsylvania-born Wright was enumerated on his ranch in the 1900 census, together with his wife, Mollie, stepdaughter, Jessie and John C. Daniels, listed as "stepfather." Wife Mollie was Mary Jane Daniels, the daughter of John Daniels and his wife Agnes (nee McKeand). The Daniels' family was enumerated at Pine Grove in the 1870 federal census.

Wife Mollie/Mary Jane was formerly the wife of William J. Taylor, who she married in 1878, and with whom she was enumerated at Mason Valley on the 1880 Census. James H. Wright and Mary J. Taylor were married December 25, 1888, at "Wright's ranch, East Walker river," in Esmeralda County. (*Walker Lake Bulletin*, 1/9/1888)

In 1902, "C. C. Bulkeley" was assessed property of the same value as Wright's had been in 1901 and Wright was not found on the 1902 assessment list. In the 1900 census, Chris C. Bulkley (27 years, born Nevada) and his wife Frances E. (31 years, born Utah) were enumerated in the Aurora Precinct, four dwellings beyond Thomas Sharpe of Fletcher Station. The young hostler and his wife had been married just two years and shared their residence with blacksmith, Byron Knerium.

Christopher C. Bulkley was the son of Albert M. Bulkley, who was a laborer in Carson City in 1870, farmed in Douglas County in 1875 and kept a hotel in Carson City as of the 1880 Census. By 1900, Albert Bulkley was a resident of Bishop, Inyo County, California.

By 1910, Christopher C. Bulkley resided on California street, in Yerington. In 1920 he lived in Sacramento with another wife, Lucy, and two daughters. He was a machinist with the Southern Pacific Railroad, at the company's shop near the Sacramento River.

Around the same time that Bulkley was shown on the ranch, the *Walker Lake Bulletin* reported that:

> "Jim Wright has sold his ranch on Walker river to John Wichman and Nate Fish. Mr. and Mrs. Wright will take a trip to the Eastern States. Wichman and Fish are young men well known in the county and are sure to succeed in their new venture." (*Walker Lake Bulletin*, 4/24/1901)

Nate Fish was the husband of Wright's other stepdaughter, May Agnes Taylor. She was the granddaughter of Agnes Daniels Compston, wife of Nevada pioneer James Compston, of Sweetwater and Smith Valley.

On the survey map of the 1903 subdivision of T8N R27E, John G. Booker showed "Buckley's House," within the southwest quarter of Section 9.

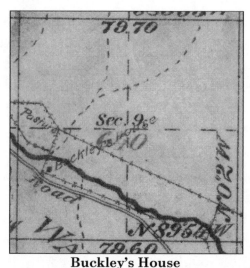

Buckley's House
(General Land Office, SW 1/4 Sec. 9, T8N R27E, M.D.M., 1903)

In the General Description of this township provided by Booker, he noted that:

> "Along the last 3 1/2 to 4 1/2 miles of its run, settlers have improved some of the land on either side [of the river] at a great expense of labor and money, and the value may be considered, of the settlers improvements in this Township, as follows:

Grulli's ranch $3,000	Wright's ranch $3,000
Morgan's ranch $4,000	Polli's [sic] ranch $10,000

As shown on Booker's map, "Buckley's House" was between the ranch of H. S. Morgan and that of Nelson Poli. J. H. Wright reappeared on the county tax assessment lists in 1903 and 1904.

In March, 1905, it was reported that "Mrs. J. Wright of East Walker, has taken her daughter, Mrs. V. B. McDaniels to Yerington for medical treatment..." (Bridgeport *Chronicle-Union*, 3/?/1905) Mrs. McDaniels was daughter Jessie Taylor. In January or February of 1906, "Miss Agnes Compston visited her sister, Mrs. Wright, at East Walker this week." (Bridgeport *Chronicle-Union*, nd. Jan.-Feb. 1906) Agnes was the daughter of James Compston and Mrs. Wright's mother, Agnes Daniels Compston, making Agnes and Mrs. Wright half-sisters.

James H. Wright acquired a federal land patent for portions of Section 9, in T8N R27E, in November of 1905. Wright's application for the patent undoubtedly preceded the patent's issuance date so that by the time it was received, Wichman and Fish owned the ranch.

The following appeared on an undated page of the Bridgeport *Chronicle-Union*, between 1907 and 1910, probably in the month of November:

> "John Wichman, formerly of Looseville has moved with his family to the old Wright ranch, on the East Walker river, which he has purchased."

James H. Wright was later enumerated on the 1910 census in the household of Harry O. Lewis in the Cambridge Precinct, and was listed as a married man, although his wife was not then in the household. Mary Wright, daughter Jessie and grandchildren Ruby B. and James

G. Paige were living in the town of Hawthorne, where Mrs. Wright operated a dairy. Ten years later, James and Mary Wright were residing together in Yerington.

Tragedy occurred on the East Walker in the summer of 1911. As reported by the Yerington *Times*, the account was given as follows:

> "Indian Girl Loses Her Life in River – Wagon Sticks in Quick Sand and Girl Is Washed From the Wagon Seat.
>
> While crossing the East Walker river at the Wichman ranch on Monday of this week a young Indian girl lost her life by drowning.
>
> The river is quite high at that point and the current swift. The woman drove into the water with a team and light wagon to make the crossing.
>
> The wagon apparently stuck in quicksand and the horse failed to pull it out, but managed to kick loose from the woman and struggle out of the water.
>
> The wagon continued to sink until the water ran over the bed. Just whether the young squaw fell out of the wagon or the bed was turned over by the current is not known, but she disappeared in the rapidly rushing stream.
>
> Soon her people were on the banks of the river looking for her, but not until several hours after the accident did they find the body, and then it was about two and a half miles down the river from where the accident happened.
>
> The young girl was a bright and intelligent young girl about 19 years of age, and had practically been raised by Mrs. George W. Webster when the Webster family resided on the ranch on the East Walker. She had been taught to be a good cook, housekeeper, etc., and the white people as well as the people of her own tribe grieve deeply at her untimely ending. The remains were taken in charge by her relatives and given a Christian burial. – Yerington *Times*." (Reno Evening *Gazette*, 7/29/1911)

Not long after Wichman took up residence on the old Wright ranch, he applied to have a post office established on his ranch for the convenience of him and his neighbors. The U. S. Postmaster established the Wichman Post Office in Mineral County, on December

6, 1911, appointing John H. Wichman as its postmaster. Mr. Wichman remained the postmaster at Wichman until 1932, at which time his wife, Mabel R. Wichman assumed the position. The county location of the Wichman post office was changed to Lyon County in March of 1933, after the State legislature approved the segregation of the area of the East Walker River from Mineral to Lyon County.

In August of 1913, a summer storm passed over the area of the East Walker:

> "Cloudburst Ruins Crops – East Walker River Section Suffers
> Severely from Terrific Storm
>
> *Special to the Gazette* – Yerington, August 19. – A cloudburst which visited the East Walker river section last Sunday did great damage to farms in that vicinity, covering many acres of valuable farm land with debris and washing away crops.
>
> At the Wichman ranch the flood was at its height. The ranch was covered to a depth of a foot with mud, sand and debris and Mrs. Wichman and her children were forced to flee for their lives through water that was knee-deep.
>
> The Wichman house was filled with mud, water running through the house six inches deep. The Poli ranch, just below [downstream of] the Wichman place, was damaged to the extent of about $1,500. Ditches were washed away and crops ruined."
> (Reno Evening *Gazette*, 8/19/1913)

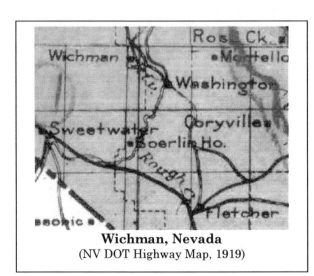

Wichman, Nevada
(NV DOT Highway Map, 1919)

By 1914 the property was assessed for taxes to "Wichman Bros." This area became known as Wichman and a post office was established there.

John and James Wichman were the sons of Jacob Wichmann and Rachael Compston, and the nephews of Sweetwater pioneer rancher, James Compston. Their parents had operated the Willow Grove Station, at the mouth of Powell Canyon near Whisky Flat, in Esmeralda (now Mineral) County. After the death and burial of their mother and their newborn baby brother, Jacob in 1881, oldest son James went with his father to attend to the toll station on the Luning to Grantsville Road, north of the town of Luning. Youngest son, John, went to live with his uncle James Compston and his wife, Agnes Daniels Compston, at Sweetwater.

James Wichman(n) never married and spent his lifetime in mining and ranching. His brother John married twice, first to Arkana "Arkie" Ball, who died eight years after the couple was married. John married again, this time to Mabel McCart, in 1911.

James Wichman died in 1946 and was buried in the Valley View Cemetery, in Yerington. John Wichman died in 1955 and was buried near his brother's grave in Yerington.

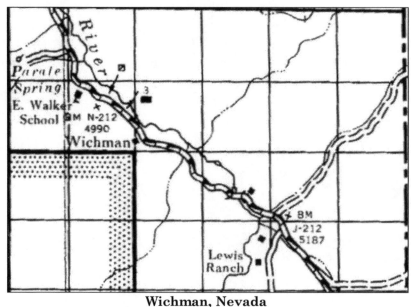

Wichman, Nevada
(NV DOT 1953 Quadrangle Map No. 2)

In 1941, after having purchased the Ira Fallon, Morgan brothers and "Polly" East Walker ranches in 1939, Major Max Fleischmann added to his East Walker River holdings. The Nevada State *Journal* wrote:

"Ranch Holdings Are Increased.

Yerington, July 31. (Special) - Major Fleischmann has increased his holdings on the East Walker River by the recent purchase of the Wichman ranch from Mr. and Mrs. John Wichman, who took possession of the property in 1907, and have since made their home there.

Major Fleischmann will operate the ranch in connection with the Morgan ranches, which he purchased about two years ago.

The Wichmans will move to Smith Valley about September 1 and will make their home on the Litser property which they recently acquired." (Nevada State *Journal*, 8/1/1941)

Chapter 10

Poli Ranch
(Est. ca. 1887; Sections 5 and 8, T8N R27E, M.D.M.)

"Nelson Polie" was first assessed for property in Esmeralda County in the year 1887, with a valuation of his holdings listed at $2,140. By 1904, the County Assessor placed a valuation on the Poli property at $4,480. In November, 1905, Nelson Poli obtained his federal land patent for portions of Sections 5 and 8, in T8N R27E.

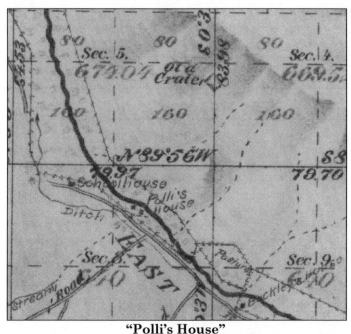

"Polli's House"
(General Land Office, NE 1/4 Sec. 9, T8N R27E, M. D. M., 1903)

Nelson Poli was married to Kate Livingston, in December of 1889, at Bodie, California. A native of Sonora, California, Miss Livingston was the sister of Julia C. McKeough, the wife of Aurora blacksmith John McKeough, and John Livingston, who also resided at Aurora.

Less than a year later, the *Walker Lake Bulletin* brought the sad tidings of the deaths of Nelson Poli's wife and newborn child, who were buried at Aurora.

> "DIED. POLI – On East Walker River, October 7, 1890, Mrs. Nelson Poli." (*Walker Lake Bulletin*, 10/22/1890)

> "DIED. POLI – On East Walker River, October 15, 1890, infant child of Mr. and Mrs. Nelson Poli." (*Ibid.*)

Three years after the death of his wife and infant child, the *Walker Lake Bulletin* advised that, "Nelson Poli has caused the removal of his wife's remains from Aurora to Sonora, Cal." Presumably the infant was buried together with Kate, as this was fairly common when a mother and newborn child deceased at a time so close to one another. (*Walker Lake Bulletin*, 10/25/1893)

Nelson Poli married again, in June, 1900, to Gertrude Swasey, the daughter of Horace and Margaret Swasey, of Wabuska in Lyon County. The couple had two children, Della M. and Daniel E. Poli, before divorcing sometime prior to 1910.

Mr. Poli was one of the East Walker River ranchers and farmers who, in 1900, protested the continuation of the toll franchise of the Southern Development Corporation, which ran the old Bodie Toll Road between Hawthorne and Aurora. Refusing to pay toll, Poli received a threat of arrest from the company, but after receiving a petition from residents, the Esmeralda County Commissioners rescinded a prior order authorizing the company's franchise. The case ultimately went to the Nevada Supreme Court, which affirmed the Commissioner's actions which made the Bodie Toll Road a public highway.

Prior to 1918, Poli's daughter Della married Ambus W. Archer. In 1922, Archer obtained a federal land patent to additional portions of sections 5 and 8, T8N R27E, adjacent to Nelson Poli's ranch. The Archer's were divorced in 1923.

Nelson Poli never remarried. He died in 1918 and is buried in an unmarked grave at the Valley View Cemetery, in Yerington. (Old cemetery listing by Mrs. Connie Rosaschi, Nevada Tombstone Transcription Project)

Nothing further was found about the Poli children. Nephew Arthur Poli moved to San Francisco sometime before 1918, when he was registered for the draft during World War I.

In 1920, the property belonging to the Estate of Nelson Poli was valued by the Mineral County Assessor at $9,635. In 1922, the "Poli Ranch" property was listed in the name of Ira Fallon, with an assessed value $4,855.

By 1924, in addition to owning the Poli Ranch, Fallon also was assessed taxes for the Webster Ranch and the Nine Mile Ranch. In 1926, Fallon was assessed for the Poli, Nine Mile, Sharpe [Fletcher] and "East Walker" ranches. These assessments continued to the year 1930, with Ira Fallon, Jr. being assessed for the Sharpe Ranch at Fletcher. The Sharpe property may have been a wedding gift from Fallon to his son, Ira, Jr., who, around 1929, married Lucille Lewis, daughter of Mr. and Mrs. Harry Lewis, who lived near Coal Valley.

In 1931, the Reno Evening *Gazette* ran an article titled, "Property Sold at Auction," in which it reported on delinquent tax sales held in several northern Nevada counties. The report included sales held at Hawthorne, by Mineral County and noted that, "Major delinquent amounts which were not offered for sale but on which suit will be brought in the interests of the county by the district attorney were: Ira Fallon, $1,192.43 and $973.24; Thomas and George Hay, $691.83 ..." (Reno Evening *Gazette*, 7/23/1931)

Fallon may have resolved his tax difficulties for some, but not all of the ranches along the East Walker owned by him, as he continued to reside "at the Fallon ranch on the East Walker." (Reno Evening *Gazette*, 1/30/1934)

Mrs. Catherine (Kate) Fallon (nee Theelan), whom Fallon had married about 1902, died in February of 1938. In November of 1938, an article involving the Fallon family noted that Mr. Fallon "now makes his home in Santa Rosa," California. (Reno Evening *Gazette*, 11/16/1938)

Ira Fallon died at his Santa Rosa home in 1940. The notice of his death that appeared in the Nevada State *Journal*, reported:

"Mr. Fallon was born at Sebastopol, Calif., March 23, 1874. He spent most of his boyhood in Forestville, California. In the early '90s he moved with his parents to a ranch in Churchill county. The ranch on which they settled is now the townsite of Fallon, which was named in their honor.

Here Mr. Fallon engaged extensively in livestock ranching, but later moved to Smith valley, where he lived for several years and, in 1911, was elected to the Nevada legislature.

From Smith Valley Fallon moved to Yerington where he bought a large sheep ranch, but later sold it and moved to Mendocino county, Calif. He remained there for some time, coming back to Nevada where he lived until 1938, at which time illness compelled him to retire to Santa Rosa. His wife, Catherine, died in Reno, in April, 1938.

Surviving him are three sons, Ira Fallon, Jr. of Riverside, California; Delbert Fallon of Minden, and Leland Fallon of Reno. Two brothers, Franklin Fallon of Victoria, B. C., and Milton E. Fallon, of Oakland." (Nevada State *Journal*, 2/22/1940)

On August 3, 1939, the Reno Evening *Gazette* reported the sale of four of the East Walker River ranches:

"Max Fleischmann Buys Ranch Holdings

Purchase of four cattle ranches in the East Walker river district by Major Max Fleischmann for $160,000 was announced today by Norman Biltz and associates, who handled the transaction.

The properties include the Ira Fallon, Morgan Brothers, Polly [sic] and Green [Nine Mile] ranch holdings and area located about thirty-five miles south of Yerington. Edward McConnell, who formerly engaged in the livestock business in the eastern part of the state, has been named manager of the holdings, it was announced. He has resided at Madera, Calif., for the past three years.

The four ranches have a total area of about 7000 acres, 1500 acres of which are under cultivation, and are the base property for nearly 250,000 acres of public domain and range land rights. The ranches were purchased from the Morgan family and the California Lands Company."

Poli Ranch
(National Agricultural Image Project (NAIP), Mitchell Spring Quadrangle, 2005)

Chapter 11

Powell Ranch
Also known as Webster Ranch and Webster's Station
(Est. ca. 1869; Section 29, T9N R27E, M.D.M.)

This place is located north of the Wichman and Poli ranches.

Powell's House
(General Land Office, T9N R27E, M.D.M., 5/19/1869)

The road with the vertical words "to Washington," to the left of Powell's house in the above view, was fully noted by the surveyor to be the "Pine Grove to Washington" road. It led south from Pine Grove to the town of Washington, in the Washington Mining District.

There is no information identified as to who Powell of "Powell's House" was, but the place was also later shown on the following map.

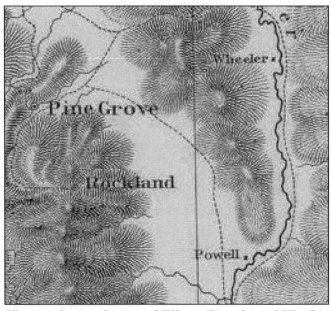

Powell's ranch, northeast of Elbow Ranch and Washington
(Topographical Map of Central California, with a part of Nevada; J. D. Whitney, 1873)

In October of 1878, the land on which Powell's house was located, being the northwest quarter of the southwest quarter of Section 29, T9N R27E, was patented by the U. S. to James A. Webster. Also acquiring land in Section 29 in the years 1891, 1905 and 1910, was George W. Webster, later known to be the owner of the Webster Ranch on the East Walker River.

In 1878, L. C. Finney leased the toll road of J. C. McTarnahan.

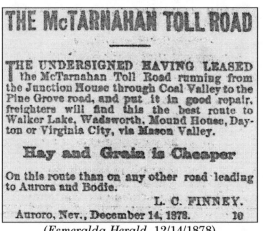

(*Esmeralda Herald*, 12/14/1878)

In 1880, the *Esmeralda Herald*, at Aurora, reported on work being done on a road. It noted that, "Lew C. Finney has a force of men working on the Virginia [City] and Aurora road between the Six Mile House and Webster's Station on Walker river..." (*Esmeralda Herald*, 8/14/1880)

The "Webster Bros." were assessed for property in 1883, no land description having been given by the County Assessor. In 1885, only Geo. W. Webster was assessed for property in Esmeralda County. By 1891, the property of G. W. Webster was valued at $5,385. In 1903, Webster's property was valued at $7,325, including real and personal property.

In March of 1905, "G. W. Webster of the Acme ranch on East Walker was in town [Bodie] Monday." (Bridgeport *Chronicle-Union*, 3/?/1905)

The Webster brothers were James Alfred and George W. Webster, natives of England who reported on the 1900 census that they had come to the United States in 1866 and 1865, respectively. In 1875, G. W. Webster (24 years, born England) was enumerated on the Nevada State Census, residing in Esmeralda County, a stock raiser by trade. Also nearby Webster's residence was thirteen year old "E. Webster," a young male whose occupation was listed as stock raiser.

Also living in Esmeralda County in 1875, were farmer "A. Webster" (52 years, born England), N. Webster (42 years, housekeeper, born England) and E. O. Webster (female, 27 years, born England). This Webster family unit was enumerated in proximity to the Schooley and Meisner families, most associated with Mason Valley. "H. Webster" (53 years, male, Cook, born England) was enumerated in Esmeralda County, but he lived near the McAfee family at Fish Lake Valley. The family of Henry and Nancy Webster, of England, comprised those Webster's living in Esmeralda County in 1875.

In 1880, Henry and Nancy's youngest son, Edwin E. Webster, was enumerated at Virginia City in the household of his brother, druggist Mark Webster, and Mark's wife Ellen. Also with these Webster's was John D. Morrow, listed as "brother-in-law," who had married their sister, Ellenor O. Webster in 1879, at Virginia City.

By this time, Henry and Nancy Webster had left Nevada and were residing at Calpella Township, in Mendocino County, California. In their household was daughter Ellenor Morrow (21 years, born England)

and granddaughter, Lizzybelle Morrow (8 months, born California). Another daughter, Annie Webster Shimmin, also resided in Mendocino County. She was wife of Robert L. Shimmin, whose father, E. R. Shimmin, had settled the nearby Shimmin Ranch, also on the East Walker River.

Back on the East Walker River in Esmeralda County, brothers James A. Webster and George W. Webster were enumerated in Pine Grove Township on the 1880 census. The two were partners in the farm they'd settled on the river. Four years later, in February 1884, George W. Webster married Ida Gertrude Willis, a native of Carmi, Illinois, at Cambridge, in Esmeralda (now Lyon) County.

Patriarch Henry Webster died in 1885, probably at Fresno, California, where sons Mark and J. A. Webster, as partners, had opened a drug store. Henry left to his several children his Fresno real property, in evenly divided parcels. In 1888, Mrs. Nancy Webster, then 60 years of age, moved from Virginia City to Fresno to reside with her children in that city.

Two years later, the Fresno Weekly *Republican* reported:

> "J. A. Webster is in receipt of a telegram announcing the death of his eldest sister, Mrs. R. D. Shinmin [sic] at Willets, Mendocino county. The remains will be brought here for burial. They will be accompanied by Mr. Webster's mother and sister." (Fresno Weekly *Republican*, 12/26/1890)

George W. and Gertrude Webster were enumerated in Cambridge precinct, Esmeralda County on the 1900 census, near after the residence of Nelson Poli. The Webster household also included daughters Lillian (15 years, born Nevada) and Violet (13 years, born Nevada). Still at Cambridge in 1910, only the Webster's daughter Lillian remained in the home of the parents.

In or around June and July, 1910, it was reported that:

> "Ira Fallon of Wellington has purchased the Geo. Webster ranch on East Walker river. Mr. Fallon recently sold his ranch at Wellington to the Hunewills of Bridgeport. Possession in both cases will be given the first of next January." (Bridgeport *Chronicle Union*, nd. June-July 1910)

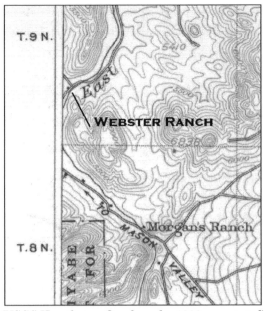

(USGS Hawthorne Quadrangle, 1909, annotated)

By the time of the 1914 tax assessments, the Webster ranch lands were listed in the name of Ira T. Fallon. In 1924, it was identified only as "East Walker" ranch, as it was on the 1930 assessment roll for Fallon's holdings. This area was annexed into Lyon County in 1933.

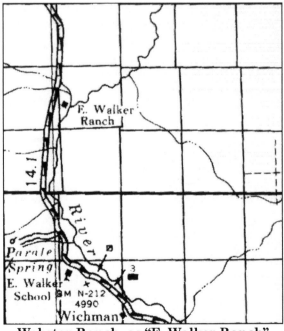

Webster Ranch, as "E. Walker Ranch"
(NV DOT Quadrangle Map No. 2, 1953)

After selling the ranch, George and Gertrude Webster moved to Yerington, where their married daughters resided. George W. Webster died in 1919 and was buried in the Valley View Cemetery, in Yerington.

Seemingly a woman of energy and intelligence, Gertrude Webster became active in the town and county life. In the mid-1920's she worked diligently toward preservation of an ancient writings site that was on the old Webster ranch property. Gertrude died in 1947 and was buried next to George at the Valley View Cemetery. The East Walker River prehistoric site she had worked to preserve was listed on the National Register of Historic Places in the 1980's.

The Calvary Cemetery, at Fresno, shelters the graves of Henry Webster (1821-1885), Nancy Webster (1822-1909), James A. Webster (1847-1931), James' wife, Caroline Payson Webster (died 1940) and his sisters, E. O. Morrow (1859-1928) and Annie W. Shimmin (1852-1890).

In the early 1930's, former Nevada Governor, James G. Scrugham wrote a column for the Nevada State *Journal*. In one column, Scrugham wrote of the area where the Webster Ranch was located:

> "In addition to the coal measures, the valley of the East Walker river contains numerous fossil beds, and some placer gold operations are now under way at the Ira Fallon place, formerly known as the Webster ranch..." (Nevada State *Journal*, 7/26/1932)

In 1939, news of the sale of four of the East Walker River ranches was reported:

> "Max Fleischmann Buys Ranch Holdings
> Purchase of four cattle ranches in the East Walker river district by Major Max Fleischmann for $160,000 was announced today by Norman Biltz and associates, who handled the transaction.
> The properties include the Ira Fallon [Webster], Morgan Brothers, Polly [sic] and Green [Nine Mile] ranch holdings and area located about thirty-five miles south of Yerington. Edward McConnell, who formerly engaged in the livestock business in the eastern part of the state, has been named manager of the holdings, it was announced. He has resided at

Madera, Calif., for the past three years.

The four ranches have a total area of about 7000 acres, 1500 acres of which are under cultivation, and are the base property for nearly 250,000 acres of public domain and range land rights. The ranches were purchased from the Morgan family and the California Lands Company." (Reno Evening *Gazette*, 8/3/1939)

Two years later, news of the loss of the ranch house was reported:

"Fire Destroys Lyon Landmark
Yerington, Jan. 6 (Special)

The ranch house on the Max Fleischman [sic] property on the East Walker burned to the ground Sunday morning, in spite of the efforts of the ranch personnel and CCC enrollees called from Camp Mason Valley. The fire is believed to have been caused by a defective flue.

The house was occupied by the manager of the ranch, Edward McConnell, and his family, and most of the furniture and personal belongings were saved.

The house has long been a landmark on the East Walker. It was built by George Webster about 1900, and when Max Fleishman bought the property a year ago, the house was remodeled and refinished." (Nevada State *Journal*, 1/7/1941)

Fleishman replaced the home that burned and it was completed in May of 1941. (Nevada State *Journal*, 5/30/1941)

According to an Abstract of Title, for the period of October 10, 1950 to January 23, 1951, Clayton E. Gunn sold the East Walker Ranches to C. C. and Eileen E. Pierce in September 1950. The Pierce's transferred the ranch properties to George Virgil Larson and his wife, Bernice, on November 1, 1950. The instrument of this transfer noted that the "deed is also subject to a certain mortgage dated January 15, 1949, executed by William D Holmes and Mary K. Holmes, his wife, to secure an indebtedness of $100,000...Dated January 14, 1949, in favor of Max C. Fleischmann..." (Washoe Title Insurance Company; copy of J. J. Connelly; on file at Mineral County Museum)

A field trip was held in November, 1952 by the Missionary Voluntary Society and the Nature Club, both possibly El Dorado County, California entities. According to the *Mountain Democrat*, the "trip led to a camp site on the East Walker Ranch, which is owned by Mr. and Mrs. Virgil Larson, and located 28 miles south of Yerrington [sic], Nevada." (*Mountain Democrat* (Placerville), 11/13/1952)

According to "Yerington Social Notes," a column in the Nevada State *Journal* of February 24, 1953, the "East Walker Ranches" were sold once more. This article reported:

> "Virgil Larson, owner of the East Walker Ranches for the past two and a half years, sold his interest to the Bigelow Logging Company of Placerville, California. Mr. and Mrs. Albert Bigelow and three daughters of Placerville will operate the ranch and make their home there. Mr. Larson has associated himself with the Bob Peterson Chevrolet Company in Yerington."

Larson purchased the "former Charlie Perry ranch" near the end of March, 1953.

In early November, 1954, the resignation of "Alexander G. Bodenstein, work unit conservationist," was reported as planned to occur on November 17th. Bodenstein was with the Mason Valley Soil Conservation Service, at its Yerington headquarters. (Reno Evening *Gazette*, 11/10/1954) The Nevada State *Journal* reported later that month that, as per the Mason Valley *News*, "Alex Bodenstein...will manage the large East Walker holding of A. Stanley Murphy." (Nevada State *Journal*, 11/17/1954) The previous September Murphy had purchased the seven ranches formerly owned by Max Fleishman.

Webster Ranch, also known as East Walker Ranch
(National Agricultural Image Project (NAIP), Mitchell Spring Quadrangle, 2005)

Poli and Webster ranches
(National Agricultural Image Project (NAIP), Mitchell Spring Quadrangle, 2005)

Chapter 12

Shimmin Ranch

(Est. ca. 1862; Section 4, T9N R27E and Section 33, T10N R33E, M.D.M.)

At the Esmeralda County Commissioners' meeting of August 1, 1864, the Board took up the matter of a citizens' petition for a County road "running from the 'Nine Mile Ranch' to Wellingtons Bridge on East Walker River." The Commissioners ordered the clerk to post three notices, "one at the 'Nine Mile Ranch,' one at 'Cottonwood' and one at 'Shermans Ranch'," to notify to interested parties that the Board was considering action in the matter. Parties in opposition were to be afforded the opportunity to state the grounds of their opposition. (Minutes, Esmeralda County Commissioners, 8/1/1864, p. 62) "Cottonwood" is probably the place formerly referred to as "Cotton Woods," in the Esmeralda Commissioners minutes in September, 1863, establishing the boundary of Township No. 1. [See at p. 4.]

At the meeting of the Commissioners in mid-August, 1864, the Board appointed election officials for Precinct No. 5, East Walker River, appointing Wm. Crauthers [sic], A. G. Sherman and Oglesby as judges, and setting the polling place to be located at "William Shimmins [sic] House." In September, the Board approved payment for election services to "E. R. Shimmins" [sic], "William Carothers" and A. G. Sherman. (Minutes, Esmeralda County Commissioners, 8/15/1864, p. 66 and 9/14/1864, pp. 71-72)

The Commissioners' established new election precincts in October 1864, including Precinct No. 5, to "comprise from Nine Mile Ranch to

Wellingtons Bridge on East Walker River and that the Polls be held in said Precinct at the house of William Shimmins [sic] and it is furthered ordered that S. Perkins, A. G. Sherman and Edward Shimmins [sic]" were appointed judges of the Election at the precinct for the ensuing year. (Minutes, Esmeralda County Commissioners, 10/4/1864, p. 76)

Two months later the Sacramento Daily *Union* began to run an advertisement titled, "Great Bargain." For sale was a ranch containing 320 acres of "Good Tillage Land, Situated on East Walker River, within thirty-eight miles of Aurora, twenty miles from Wellington's Station." The ad also noted the availability of an "Excellent Water Power," with a "Central-discharge Wheel; two Arastras and Crusher; building 43 x 21 feet, and 600 feet in a Quartz Lode within a mile and a half of the Mill." Interested parties were to contact Charles Gilman, at Virginia City, or A. G. Sherman, on the premises. (Sacramento *Daily Union*, 12/13/1864) The ad ran until late January, 1865.

A. G. Sherman was Albert Gallatin Sherman, a native of Massachusetts, born about 1808. In 1861, he was included in the San Francisco City Directory, and was listed as a Commission merchant residing on Union Street, near Polk Street. A. G. Sherman died at the age of 63 years of age on July 14, 1871, in San Francisco.

No deed from either A. G. Sherman or Charles Gilman transferring ownership in the above described property was found in the records of Esmeralda County. A chattel deed recorded December 12, 1864 was on record between D. T. Lufkin and George B. Harnett as grantors and

Isaac Lankershim, John Tormey, Peter Fagan [sic], William B. Storey and A. G. Sherman as grantees. (Email from Lois Skullestad, Esmeralda County Recorder's Office, 8/2/2013) The deed did not involve any real estate, but personal property in the way of milling equipment similar to that described in the above advertisement. This may have been a financing document for what was referred to as the "Pine Creek Mill Co. and sometimes known as and called the Brodie [sic] Mill Co."

In May of 1863, a correspondent writing from Aurora to the Daily *Alta California* about matters in the mining town mentioned that ore from the Red, White and Blue mine, at Aurora, was being crushed by the Bodie Mill, "owned by Messrs. Lufkin, Lake & Co." (Daily *Alta California*, 5/16/1863) The Pine Creek mill was variously known as "either the Dows; Bodies; or Brodie's; Story's [sic] and Lufkins." It had ten stamps, was built at a cost of $40,000 and was "located in Del Monte Canyon." (*An 1864 Directory and Guide to Nevada's Aurora*, Clifford Alpheus Shaw, 2006, p. 128)

There is no way to definitively determine if the milling equipment offered for sale with the ranch land by A. G. Sherman in late 1864 was the same mill as the Bodie or Pine Creek Mill noted in the Lufkin and Harnett deed, but that deed was the only instrument found of record bearing Sherman's name.

According to a correspondent from Aurora writing to the Sacramento newspaper, the "parties that bought the Pine Creek mill are here and are preparing to take it to the new district near Walker river..." (Sacramento Daily *Union*, 12/5/1866) The "Bodie Mill, at Aurora" was later purchased by "Messrs. Cheever, Pray and Todman," who planned to move it to the Walker River district. (Daily *Alta California*, 12/8/1866) By April, 1867, favorable reports continued to come in "from Pine Grove and Washington Districts, near Walker river," where "Captain Cheever's mill" on the last cleaning up, had netted some $65 to the ton. (Daily *Alta California*, 4/6/1867)

The mill equipment offered by Sherman in 1864 was seemingly located somewhere along the East Walker River. The Pine Creek or Bodie Mill was located in Del Monte Canyon. If these locations are given accurately, it would be difficult to say that it was the same equipment. Who, then, actually ended up with the 320 acre ranch and mill offered for sale in 1864? This question is yet unanswered.

As he had written to the San Francisco *Bulletin* about the Gold Hill Range and Mineral City, J. Ross Browne also wrote of his stay at "Shimmen's Ranch" in the summer of 1864. He located Shimmin's house to be in the "vicinity of Lookout Mountain, a point about two miles above [upstream or south of] Mineral City." Browne noted his stay with Mr. Shimmens [sic], who 'within two years...has surrounded himself with most of the comforts of a civilized house." (San Francisco *Bulletin*, 1/25/1865)

In the 1865 *Harper's New Monthly Magazine* article, Browne also mentioned "Shimmen's Ranch," in his discussion of places and features that he had seen on his tour along the East Walker River. This was the ranch of William E. Shimmin, brother-in-law of Isaac N. Farwell, the latter of whom was once the Esmeralda County Clerk when the county seat was at Aurora and also when at Hawthorne.

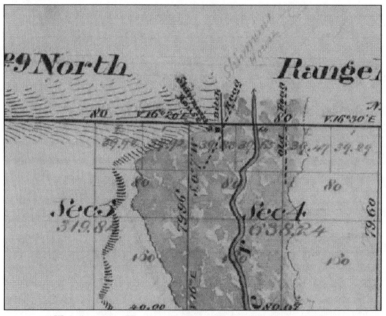

"Shimmons House," near East Walker River
(General Land Office Map, Section 4, T9N R27E, M.D.M., 1869)

The survey field notes of the north boundary line survey for Township 9 North, Range 27 East, identified the corner common to Sections 4 and 5 of T9N, and sections 33 and 32 of T10N, in R27E, the latter sections being immediately north of the former sections. The surveyors noted the way in which they marked the location of the corner and referenced that "W Shimmins [sic] house bears S. 3/4 E" and "SW cor of E. R. Shimmins [sic] house bears S 81 1/2 E dist about 11 chains," from the corner marker. These men were brothers William E. Shimmin and Edward R. Shimmin.

A native of Isle of Man, older brother William E. Shimmin was born about the year 1816. He was the son of William Shimmin and Mary Maria Stephens. The family immigrated to America sometime between 1825 and 1835. The first American-born child of the William and Mary Shimmin family was Robert E. Shimmin, who was born about 1835 in Indiana. Their youngest son, Thomas W. Shimmin, was born about a year later in Michigan. In 1850, the main Shimmin family resided at Seward, in Winnebago County, Illinois.

By the time of the 1850 census enumeration, William E. Shimmin was living at Arena, in nearby Iowa County, Wisconsin, together with his wife, Wealthy (Welthy) Paul Farwell, and the couple's son, Francis, aged 4 years. This branch of the Shimmin family remained at Arena to the 1860 census enumeration, where William successfully farmed and the family continued to grow in size.

William E. Shimmin's brother, Edward Robert Shimmin married Susan Maria Robinson, the daughter of local Seward farmer Richard Robinson and his wife, the former Susan Durbin. Edward and Susan Shimmin had one daughter, Sarah J. Shimmin (born 1849) and two sons, Richard W. (born 1848) and Robert L. Shimmin (born 1853). Mother Susan Robinson Shimmin died in February 1853, and was buried in the Twelve Mile Grove Cemetery, at Seward, Illinois.

According to the minutes of the Mono County Board of Supervisors in September 1861, Wm. E. Shimmins, together with Joseph Webster was appointed as a "viewer" of the street the citizens of Aurora had petitioned to be opened "from (the) vicinity of (the) Pioneer Mill towards Esmeralda Gulch." (Minutes, Mono County Board of Supervisors, Sept. 2, 1861, unnumbered page)

In May of 1863, the Postmaster of the Post Office, in Sacramento, California advertised the letters that were waiting to be picked up, and named W. E. "Shimmins" as one who had received correspondence.

In the new State of Nevada, in 1865, the Internal Revenue Service assessed income taxes to Wm. E. "Shimmins" at Carson Valley and in 1866 a Wm. E. "Shimmins" was taxed for income, listing his residence as being at Genoa, in the Carson Valley.

119

Also assessed for income taxes in Nevada in the month of May, 1865, was A. D. Robinson and Co., at Carson Valley, for an income of $241 and a tax of $6.75. This was Amos D. Robinson, son of Richard and Susan Robinson, and brother-in-law of William E. and Edward R. Shimmin. In January of 1868, Alice Maria Robinson, the daughter of A. D. and S. A. Robinson, aged fifteen years of age, died and was buried in the Pine Grove Cemetery, then in Esmeralda (now Lyon) County, south of Yerington, Nevada.

In November, 1869, Edward R. Shimmin began to serve one term in the Nevada State Assembly, representing Esmeralda County. (*Political History of Nevada*; Heller, 1996, p. 160) Assemblyman Shimmin's round trip mileage between his home and the Capitol was 160 miles, for which he was paid $64.00 in 1869. (*Journal of the Assembly, Fourth Session, Legislature of the State of Nevada*, 1869; p. 14) In this same session, Shimmin served on the Assembly Committees on Federal Relations, Agriculture, Military and Indian Affairs and Swamped and Overflowed Lands.

On the 24th day of the Session, Mr. Shimmin "gave notice that he would on some future day introduce a preamble and resolution in relation to the Indian Reservation situated in Esmeralda County," which he did on the 51st day of the legislative session as Assembly Joint Resolution No. 31. The resolution asked that the Walker River Indian Reservation lands for 8 miles from the north end of Walker Lake be opened to settlement.

Two days later the Standing Committee on Federal Relations reported back on AJR 31, recommending its passage. It was ordered engrossed on February 25, 1869. (*Journal of the Assembly, Fourth Session, Legislature of the State of Nevada*, 1869; pp. 18, 23, 26, 74, 188 and 207)

In 1868, Amos D. Robinson's parents, Richard and Susan resided in the town of Santa Clara, California, where Mr. Robinson was registered to vote. The census of 1870 enumerated the family of "A. Robinson," at Pine Grove, Nevada, including wife Sarah, "W. Robinson" (15 years, male, born Illinois) and Walter Robinson (16 years, born Illinois).

The 1870 census of Santa Clara, California included the household of farmer Richard "Robertson" [sic], including Susan Robertson and Richard W. "Shimmon" (21 years, born Illinois) and Robert L. Shimmon (17 years, born Illinois). The latter were the sons of Edward R. Shimmin and his late wife, Susan Maria Robinson. This was the last documented record of 70 year old Richard Robinson, either in California or Nevada.

By the time of the 1870 census, the William E. Shimmin family was residing at Little Lake, Mendocino County, California, and then included Nevada-born daughter Wealthy Shimmin, aged 2 years. Mr. Shimmin was listed as a farmer on this census.

In 1880, William F. Shimmin and his mother, Wealthy and others, including Wealthy's father, Isaac Farwell, were residing in Fresno, California. W. E. Shimmin, then aged 64 year, was enumerated in the 1880 census at Whatcom, Skagit Mining District, Washington Territory. Listed as a married man, he was working as a miner.

In the subscribed biography in the *History of San Luis Obispo County, California* (1917), W. E. Shimmin's other son, Marion Shimmin wrote:

> "Mr. Shimmin's father was William Edward Shimmin, a
> native of the Isle of Man who, in 1850, joined one of the great
> ox-team trains crossing the desert wastes, came to and mined
> in Nevada, and finally reached California. While he was in
> Esmeralda county, Nevada, he discovered, with Brawley [sic],
> the Aurora mines, and was one of the men first to put a pick
> into the famous Garibaldi. He made and lost several fortunes,
> went back and forth between the West and the East, and in the
> end sent for his family, who arrived in San Francisco, via
> Panama, April 19, 1863."

Despite what was stated above, it is <u>not fact</u> that Shimmin was a co-discoverer of the Aurora mines in 1860. The history of the Esmeralda discovery by E. R. Hicks, James M. Cory and James M. Braly, is well documented, and Shimmin's name has never, before this 1917 mention, been associated with it. The names W. E. "Shimmen" and W. E. "Shimmins", however, are both listed by Cliff Shaw in his work, *An 1864 Directory and Guide to Nevada's Aurora* (2006), as having been registered to vote in Aurora, Mono County, California in 1861. He was also listed at Aurora in the Second Directory of Nevada Territory (1863), and as an assessed taxpayer on the 1863 Mono County tax roll.

Similar to Marion Shimmin's subscribed biography, the biography of Robert E. Shimmin, a grandson of Edward R. Shimmin, appeared in Volume 3 of *California and Californians* (Hunt, 1932), in which was written:

> "His grandfather, Edward Robert Shimmin, brought his family west from Illinois and settled in California in 1866. Edward Robert Shimmin was always much interested in politics, and he was one of the founders of the City of Willits in Mendocino County. The father of Robert E. Shimmin was Robert Larue Shimmin, who was born in Illinois and was a boy when the family crossed the plains to Nevada and later settled in the Santa Clara Valley in California, where he completed his education in Santa Clara College. For thirty years he was engaged in stock ranching in Mendocino County. Robert Larue Shimmin married Anna Webster, who was born in London, England."

Robert L. Shimmin was married to Annie Webster in Virginia City, Nevada on June 29, 1879, indicating he remained involved in Nevada affairs.

In 1874, relative Amos D. Robinson was appointed Postmaster at Pine Grove, Nevada. That same year one of the Shimmin men was nominated at the Esmeralda Republican County Convention to run for the office Superintendent of Schools for Esmeralda County, a race that was lost to H. D. Fletcher. The A. D. Robinson family was enumerated at Pine Grove, on the Nevada State Census of 1875.

Also in this 1875 State census was the enumeration of R. W. Shimmin, R. L. Shimmin and female S. Robinson, presumed to be mother-in-law Susan Robinson. A review of the census list in the Appendix to Journals of Senate and Assembly, published in 1877, reveals that the Shimmin brothers and Mrs. Robinson were enumerated after the residence of stock raiser W. W. Wheeler, located north of their ranch, and prior to G. W. Webster, southwest of the Shimmins, each of whom is known to have resided on the East Walker River over subsequent years. (Appendix to Journals of Senate and Assembly of the Eighth Session of the Legislature of the State of Nevada, Vol. 2, 1877, p. 99)

According to the Bodie Weekly *Standard*, in November of 1877 the "stable of Robert Shimman [sic], on East Walker river, was burned a few days ago, together with a pair of valuable young horses, some hay and grain, etc., entailing a loss of $800." (Bodie Weekly Standard, 11/21/1877) This was Robert L. Shimmin, son of Edward R. Shimmin.

On October 1, 1879, the United States General Land Office issued a land patent to Susan Robinson for portions of Section 4, T9N R27E and Section 33, T10N R27E. (Homestead Certificate No. 94, Application No. 72, Carson City, Nevada) In 1919, another patent was issued in lieu of the October 1879 patent which had an error in legal description. This corrected patent was issued to "Susan Robinson, widow of Richard Robinson," although it is certain that Susan had predeceased the issuance date of the patent. (BLM General Land Office Records) This transaction tends to indicate that the ranch was perhaps not owned by Richard W. or Robert L. Shimmin, but rather by their grandmother, Susan Robinson.

Also, in 1879, a deed transaction between Susan Robinson, as grantor, and Sweetwater's Henry Williams, as grantee, was recorded on February 17, 1879. It is believed this was the sale of the ranch and land identified in 1864 by J. Ross Browne as "Shimmen's Ranch."

In 1880, former Pine Grove postmaster Amos D. Robinson continued to reside in that town and a new daughter, Ida M. Robinson (age 7 years, born Nevada) had been added to the family home.

By this same year's census, Richard W. Shimmin and his wife, Rosetta and two daughters, Gracie and Bertha, were residing in Long Valley, Mendocino County, California. Grandmother, Susan Robinson, then 74 years of age, also resided with Richard's family.

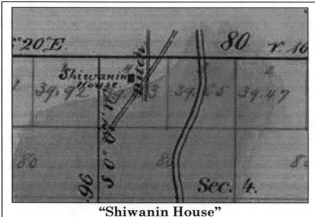

"Shiwanin House"
(General Land Office Map, T9N R27E, M.D.M., 1890)

Even though the federal government had surveyed and platted the location of "Shimmons House" in 1869, the area was resurveyed in 1890 and the government issued yet another map which showed it as "Shiwanin House."

As previously written, Sweetwater pioneer rancher, Henry Williams, who is buried at the Aurora Cemetery, purchased the Shimmin or Robinson ranch in 1879. After the deaths of Williams and his wife, Mary, the surviving executor of the estate began to sell Williams' properties, as authorized by the Probate Court. In a Notice published in the *Walker Lake Bulletin* of May 25, 1892, one of those properties was described as follows:

> "...those several tracts of land situated on lower East Walker River in the vicinity of Cambridge and known as the Shimmins [sic] or Williams ranch, and containing about 1,878.87 acres or thereabouts, together with the improvements thereon, to Peter Latapie and Bertrand Salles of the city and county of San Francisco, State of California, for the sum of $10,900.00..."

Not all of the land acquired by Latapie and Salles in the above total acreage represented the Shimmin ranch. Mrs. Susan Robinson's original acreage only amounted to about 160 acres.

Pierre Latapie, also known as Peter, and Bertrand Salles were Frenchmen and brothers-in-law who had formed a company in San Francisco in 1889, and owned a wholesale butcher establishment there. The ranch land on the East Walker River was likely a business venture and the pair is known to have run sheep on this ranch.

In 1905, Salles and Latapie purchased the Huntoon Ranch, located near Bridgeport, in Mono County, California. The partnership dissolved in 1910, and Pierre Latapie later died in San Francisco in 1919.

Bertrand Salles was assessed for the property once known as the "Shimmins or Williams ranch," in the year 1914. This was a time when this area was still in Mineral County, before it was annexed into Lyon County, around 1933. Salles was consistently assessed taxes both for the portions of Section 4, T9N R27E and Section 33, T10N R27E, until at least the year 1930. Mr. Salles died March 21, 1932 at the French Hospital, in San Francisco. He was interred at Holy Cross Cemetery, in Colma, California.

The *Mining Reporter* published an interesting article submitted to it by R. R. MacLeod regarding "The Chipmunk Gold Belt, Nevada."

MacLeod's comments provided the following insight into the area of the ranch:

"On my first trip to the Yerington copper belt I was shown a fine specimen of gold-bearing hematite ore from Chipmunk Springs, Nevada, that excited my curiosity and desire to visit the locality...

A 30-mile southerly drive from Yerington brought me to the Latapie ranch on East Walker river. Here I found the relic of an old Chilian mill, consisting of a solid diestone of granite, 5 feet in diameter, and one crushing wheel of solid granite of about the same size; the other wheel had been broken up several years ago for material with which to construct a wall. This mill was constructed and operated in the fifties, but was later replaced by a two-stamp mill, the partly-decayed mortar blocks of which still stand by the ditch near the ranch house...

A six-mile southeasterly drive from the Latapie ranch brought me to Chipmunk Springs. This is at an elevation 6,400 feet above sea level and at about the center of the gold belt that is seven miles wide by 12 miles long covering the west slope of Walker range (between it and the East Walker river)..." (*Mining Reporter*, Vol. LVI, No. 1, July 4, 1907, p. 7)

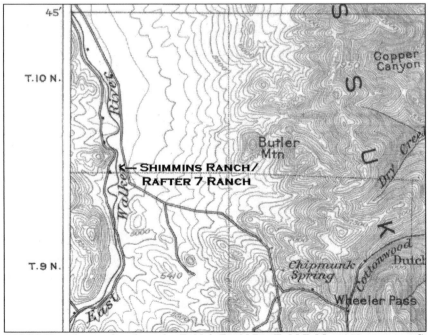

(USGS Hawthorne Quadrangle, T9N & T10N R27E, M.D.M., 1909; annotated)

In 1909, the U.S. Geological Survey produced the first Hawthorne topographic quadrangle map, shown above. Although the location of Shimmin's ranch was not named, a feature at its location was shown on it, as was the location of Chipmunk Spring in relation to it.

In 1951, the Reno Evening *Gazette* reported on the sale of Mason Valley ranches:

> "Mason Ranches Reported Sold. Four properties Placed on the List
>
> Four large ranches in the Mason valley area of Nevada, were sold to southern California people last week, says the Mason Valley news... Roland [sic] Eckis and Earl [sic] Rodi have purchased the old Silas [sic] ranch owned by A. C. Alhswede. The ranch is located on the East Walker river..." (Reno Evening *Gazette*, 1/25/1951)

In October of 1950, Rollin P. Eckis and Carl D. Rodi of Los Angeles, had purchased the "Miller [sic] Brothers vast land holdings in Sweetwater," comprised of some 4,200 acres. The Sweetwater property "formerly owned by the Yparraguierri [sic] family is one of the oldest ranches in Nevada." (Reno Evening *Gazette*, 10/28/1950) Purchasing the old Salles ranch, formerly the Shimmin Ranch, a year later, gave these California men control of some of the oldest operating ranches in Lyon County. Rodi was an attorney and Rollin Eckis went on to become the president of the Richfield Oil Company.

The "Miller Brothers" was actually the Muller Brothers, Walter and Frank. In addition to the Sweetwater Ranch [Yparraguirre], which they'd purchased sometime after September, 1939 from Tom Williams, the brothers also owned the Flying M Ranch. (Tom Williams had been injured by being kicked in the head by a horse. He died in Los Angeles in August of 1940, though the incident was not cited to be the cause of death.)

The sons of Jacob Muller and Wilhelmina Altman, pioneers of the Cahuenga Valley in Los Angeles, Walter and Frank Muller's family residence was located at what later became Sunset Blvd. in the new town of "Hollywood Land," now just Hollywood.

The enterprising young men saw the need for necessary services to offer to the stars and others flocking to the emerging entertainment capitol. They opened a high class service station that eventually grew into full automobile services and a Chrysler dealership. This and other later entrepreneurial efforts made them multi-millionaires.

Walter Muller died in 1961 and Frank died in 1972, after hosting President Richard Nixon, Vice President Spiro Agnew and others on his 85 foot luxury yacht, the Mojo.

In 1953, a 25th wedding anniversary party was held in Yerington to honor Mr. and Mrs. Harry Forbush. An article about the party appeared in the Reno Evening *Gazette* which, in part, stated that, "Mr. and Mrs. Forbush and Elmer Forbush operated a ranch in the Perry district for many years, later making their home on the Salas [sic] ranch on east Walker." It noted that about "ten years ago they sold their ranching interests in Mason valley and later moved to Fallon..." (Reno Evening *Gazette*, 11/5/1953) It isn't clear from this mention of the Salles ranch if the Forbush brothers owned the ranch or merely operated it.

The Shimmin (or Robinson) ranch is today known as the Rafter 7 Ranch. It was purchased by the Edwin L. Weigand Trust in 1989 to facilitate "charitable programs." In *The Valleys of the Walker Rivers* (Matheus, 1995), the author wrote about this ranch as follows:

> "Rafter 7 Ranch, once known as the Old Silas [sic] Ranch, was owned by several people. One of the later owners was the Oro Wheat Company ad [sic] was run by Herman Dryer. This ranch is now a retreat for vacationing priests and nuns. A special breed of sheep are raised experimental there. This is owned and operated by the E. L. Weigand Foundation." (p. 65)

Mrs. Matheus' reference to the "Old Silas Ranch" is a corruption of the name Salles, for the time that Bertrand Salles and Peter Latapie owned the old Shimmin's ranch. Her mention of the ownership of the ranch by the "Oro Wheat Company," speaks of the purchase of the ranch by "Herman L. Dreyer of Los Angeles, president of the Oroweat Bread Co.," who acquired the A-Bar-A Ranch from Mr. and Mrs. Ahlswede in January of 1951. Dreyer had paid $215,000 for the ranch and the price included 300 head of Hereford cattle. (Nevada State *Journal*, 1/31/1951)

The E. L. Weigand Foundation continued in ownership until the spring of 2013. It was purchased in this year by a nonprofit organization known as the National Fish and Wildlife Federation.

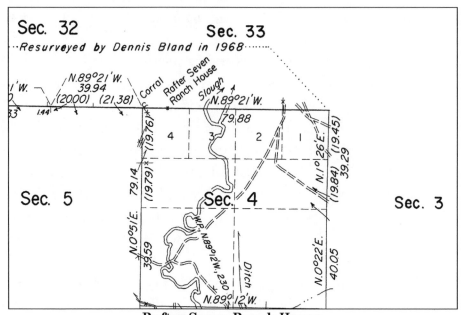

Rafter Seven Ranch House
(BLM Map, Section 4, T9N R27E, M.D.M., 1971)

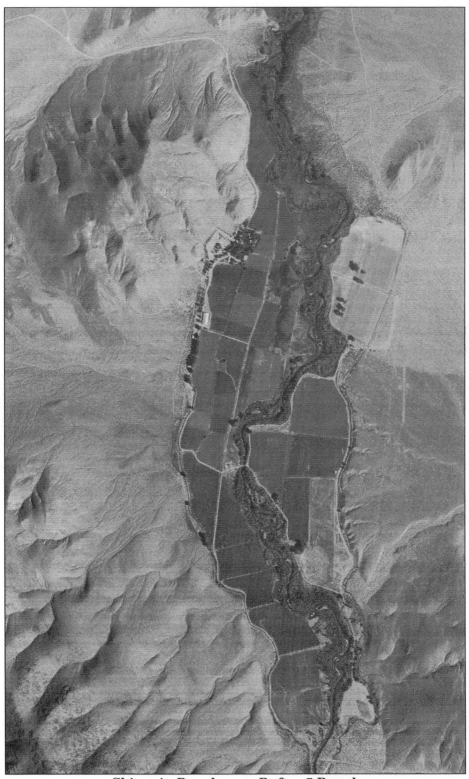

Shimmin Ranch, now Rafter 7 Ranch
(National Agricultural Image Project (NAIP), Butler Mtn., 2005)

East Walker River running through the Rafter 7 Ranch

Chapter 13

Durant's Mill
Also known as Granite City, Mineral City, Wheeler Ranch and Santa Margarita Ranch
(Est. 1861-1862; north of Shimmin's Ranch)

Just about a year and half after the mineral discoveries in the Esmeralda Mining District, and the founding of the town of Aurora in the late summer of 1860, a news item appeared in the Sacramento Daily *Union* in December of 1861, which spoke of a new mining district adjacent to the East Fork of the Walker River. Identified as called the "Walker River Mining District," the paper also reported that a second new district, called the Pacific Coal District, had also been laid out.

Of the Walker River mining district, the *Union* quoted an article, originally from the *Silver Age* newspaper, in Carson City:

> "In the mining district a number of paying quartz ledges exist, of which several have been opened quite extensively, and some of them found sufficiently rich to pay well. In consequence of this, mills are being put up on the river for crushing the rock, which pays, taking the entire mass, from $25 to $100 per ton. With one exception, the mills are on a small scale, being built more with a view to thoroughly testing the rock than to extensive working at present. The parties are generally persons of small means, and unable to put up large works, even if disposed to do so at this time. But they are satisfied that if a thorough prospecting proves their claims to be rich, there will be no trouble in getting large mills erected,

as capitalists are ready to give all the aid required after they are assured that mills will pay.

The first mill on the river below [downstream and north of] Elbow Ranch and the point where the Aurora road passes, is that of Wolland. It is 25 miles below Elbow. The frame is up and the work going on. The next is Welburn & Van Horn's, one mile further down. It is a small mill, consisting of only three arastras driven by water. A little further down is a Chile mill owned by Capt. Moore. It is worked by horse-power, driving two wheels, and is now in operation.

And still further down is the mill of S. F. Trust and Mining Company, being put up under the superintendence of Rev. Henry Durand, Principal of the Oakland College. The Trustees of that Institution having given Mr. Durand a furlough of one year to recruit his health, he concluded to devote his time entirely to out-door pursuits. Hearing much of the mines in the Mono country, he paid them a visit; and having a good opinion of the Walker river district determined to put up a mill and carry on quartz mining there. He is the pioneer in the business in that region and deserves to succeed, as there is every prospect that he will do. His mill, which is a first class one, will be ready to commence operations in about one month. It is his purpose to devote the proceeds of his labors during the year to the building up of the College, now one of the best literary institutions on the Pacific, and of which he was the founder. His mill is driven by water and works the Howland batteries. Mr. Durand has taken several quartz veins near by, some of which are known to be valuable, so that his enterprise can hardly fail to turn out a paying one in the end." (Sacramento Daily *Union*, 12/12/1861)

Granite City

At the location of Reverend Durand's mill, the article noted:

"They have laid out a town on the river and named it Granite City. The granite is there already and the "city" is expected to be by-and-bye. Of course, people abroad would fail to duly appreciate the place without the city addition. There are several frame houses already up and several cabins built of willows, mud, stone, etc. For covering the tule is largely used.

The lumber for both houses and mills is all brought from the timber lands, 30 miles higher up on the Walker. All the land along the river, between Granite City and Elbow Ranch has been taken up, as well as most of the available water-powers, many of the latter being valuable. Some of the land is also worth a good deal for pasture or tillage. Many spots, with irrigation, produce fine vegetables, there having been enough raised this season for home consumption. Potatoes, turnips, cabbage, tomatoes, etc., all do well; as much hay has also been cut as will be required in the neighborhood. There has been no snow in this District, except on the mountains, this winter. They never have more than six or eight inches of snow, according to the statement of the Indians, any season, so that stock require no feed even in the winter. There is some willows and plenty of the pine-nut 5 or 6 miles distant on the mountains. There are a good many Indians about, but they are civil and industrious, always behaving well and willing to work at anything they can do." (Sacramento Daily *Union*, 12/12/1861)

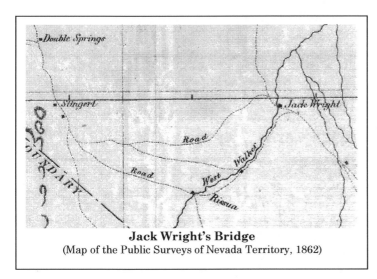

Jack Wright's Bridge
(Map of the Public Surveys of Nevada Territory, 1862)

Granite City, the *Silver Age* wrote, could be reached going from Carson City, by taking the Mono road, leaving that road at Jack Wright's bridge, and "bearing off to the left, over the valley of the West Walker, [it] passes through a low place in the hills on its east side; 50 miles from the bridge by this route brings him to Granite City, the principal camp in the District." (Sacramento Daily *Union*, 12/12/1861)

The route from Wright's bridge led east through lower Smith Valley, along the plain, toward the East Walker River, south of Wilson Canyon. Part of this route may have been used by George Wellington in 1864 for his Wellington to Reese River Toll Road.

The "Chile mill" mentioned in the above article as owned by Capt. Moore, was the same "old Chilian mill" that was noted by R. R. MacLeod, in 1907, as located on the Latapie (Shimmin) ranch. [See Chapter 12, Shimmin Ranch, p. 125.] MacLeod also noted the granite rocks used in the construction of the Chilian mill, making the area consistent with that described as the location of Granite City.

On February 1, 1862, the San Francisco *Bulletin* recapped information it had received "from Mono and Esmeralda." Included in its news item was information about recent flooding and mines in the vicinity. The article reported that:

> "All the mills are paying beyond expectation. Dervant's [sic] mill and Wilburn's arrastras, driven by water on the East Walker, 30 miles north of Aurora, had been doing well, prior to the storm..."

A month and a half later, a correspondent writing to the Daily *Alta California*, from Aurora on February 7, 1862, reported on weather conditions and impassable roads that resulted from the winter season's storms. A storm had occurred about the 14th of January and snow had "piled up in some parts 20 and 30 feet, covering up teams so that they could not be got out, and men and animals were driven to seek for shelter. After a few days interval, a terrific rain-storm set in – a perfect "deluge," continuing for six days.... One bridge on the Walker was tumbled over and went down the river."

In addition, the Aurora resident sent news about flooding on the "Walker River," and damages to homes, fields and livestock.

> "We have had dreadful accounts from Walker river. Low's ranch is entirely under water, and a great many of his stock destroyed, and his hay all gone. His house was filled with water four feet above the floor. The house is two feet six inches above ground, on a high part of the farm. Myers' ranch is still worse off – everything gone.
>
> Marsh's house was carried down the river, with two men, who barely escaped with their lives; they were safely landed about ten miles below; they had all the grub along, whisky included, so had a good time generally on the water. On leaving, they pre-empted the land on which their "ark" rested,

and have called the farm Mount Arrarat [sic]. They have employed their time, since, in securing all the hay that is floating down the river, and they calculate their piles are made, as hay is worth $250 a ton, and scare at that. They report all the stock grazing on the bottom land on the Walker, gone, drowned or starved.

As the whole valley is a sheet of water, the miners along all the banks had to take to the hills, few saving anything. They are now suffering great privations, as some have come into Aurora in awful plight." (Daily *Alta California*, 2/22/1862)

The letter also provided information about what was on "Walker's River Before the Flood":

"Everything looked bright and cheering. Rich discoveries of quartz have been made, yielding from $100 to $450 a ton, and some mills are erected. The Rev. Henry Durand [sic], Principal of the Oakland College, has put up a water power mill, working the Howland batteries. His mill was to be finished by the 1st and ready to commence operations. He has given all his time to get everything in ship shape order, and devotes the proceeds of his labor to the College which he founded in Oakland. He has also taken up some quartz veins near the location where he has erected his mill, and which are said to prospect very rich.

Van Horn's mill is a small water-power of three arastras. Wolland's mill is also small. Moore's mill is small, driven by horsepower, and has plenty of work on hand. We trust to bear favorable news when the roads get in fine traveling condition. The weather is fine, cold and bracing to-day, with every one in good spirits. [signed] Quartz." (Daily *Alta California*, 2/22/1862)

No further correspondence about the flooding was located regarding the condition of the mills along the East Walker River, after the above article.

The following May (1862), the Sacramento Daily *Union* reprinted an article titled, "The Mines at East Walker River," that had first appeared in the *Silver Age* on May 24th:

"Of the mines on the East Walker but little has been said heretofore, and yet they are deserving of as favorable mention, if we are correctly informed, as any other new mines on the eastern slope. They are located on the east branch of Walker river, between this city and Aurora; some thirty miles from the latter place and about sixty miles from Carson. From this place there are three routes to them, the nearest of which is sixty miles, and is by way of a trail crossing the Carson river at Cook's ranch, five miles from town; thence to the Hot Springs; thence to Wheeler's ranch, four miles above the junction of the East and West Walker, and thence east fifteen miles to the mines.

There are two good wagon roads leading to them, by which they can be reached in a distance of seventy-five miles, and an abundance of first rate feed and water, it is said, can be obtained on either side of the roads. One is by way of Fort Churchill, Mason's and Wheeler's; and the other by the Esmeralda road to Wright's bridge, and thence down the river fifteen miles to Smith's ranch, from which point the mines are distant twenty miles, east. The distance is about the same over each of the wagon roads.

Thus far only a limited amount of work has been done in these diggings, owing to the lack of the necessary mills to crush the rock. There are only about forty miners in the district, yet there are some seventy-five or one hundred ledges taken up, nearly every one of which prospects well in free gold; in fact, the miners have sought for nothing but gold, and have not turned their attention to silver rock. It is represented to us that they hardly consider a ledge worth locating unless the gold is visible to the naked eye, and they never take up anything unless the rock will yield a good prospect in gold after being pounded up in a mortar. The ledges vary in width from one to four feet, and show the gold from the croppings down, growing better as the distance increases. The deepest shaft that has been sunk is only forty feet, and it was from this shaft we saw the richest specimen.

Those ledges which are now claimed extend a distance of three miles from the river and are some six or seven miles in length along the river, in which are there is said to be numerous favorable mill sites, so located that they are entirely free from danger of any overflow; and within a distance of four miles there is an abundance of good pine nut timber for firewood, among which there is some suitable for building purposes, and within twelve miles of the mines there is timber for all purposes. The miners all think they have a good thing, and are awaiting the arrival of capitalist who will erect the necessary mills. (Sacramento Daily *Union*, 5/27/1862)

The article made no mention of "Durand's" or the other mills that are known to have earlier existed along this stretch of the East Walker River, but did note that the mill sites would be "entirely free from danger of any overflow." It is obvious from this comment, that the earlier mills may have suffered damage during the winter storm of the previous January.

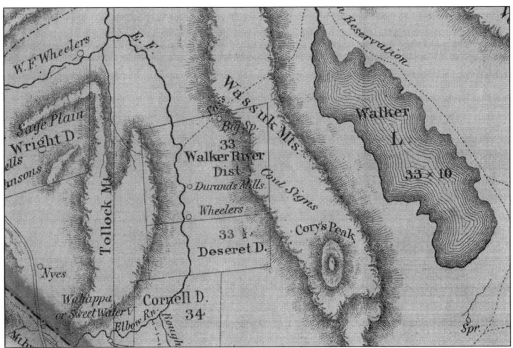

"Durand's Mills", East Walker River, Walker River Mining District
(DeGroot's Map of Nevada Territory; Warren Holt, 1863)

The site of "Durands Mills" is shown in the map view above, although the location may not have been shown in the exact place, since at this time no formal survey had been done detailing the true meander of the length of the river. The survey or compilation of this 1863 map likely took place in 1862, before it was published.

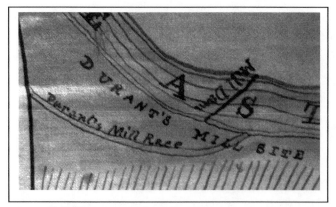

Durant's mill site location was mentioned in the minutes of the Esmeralda Board of Commissioners in 1864. The item noted was in relation to an election precinct the Board ordered "established at East Walker River" and it determined that the poll was "to be held at ~~Sherman~~ Durants Quatz [sic] Mill." A. G. Sherman was appointed to be the Inspector of the election and Wm. O. Carrothers and – Oglesby were appointed as judges of the election. (Minutes, Esmeralda County Commissioners, 1/8/1864, p. 25) Later in the year, other election precinct orders were made in relation to the precinct located on the East Walker River and are mentioned in the chapter on the Shimmin Ranch.

In October, 1864, the Sacramento Daily *Union* reported that the newspaper at Aurora had written:

> "J. Ross Browne, who has been on a visit to the East Walker River Mining District, returned to Aurora a few days since, bringing with him one of the most remarkable petrifactions we ever saw or heard of. It is that of a piece of wood about fifteen inches long and about four in thickness, apparently pine, which is not only thoroughly petrified, but is also thoroughly impregnated with iron..." (Sacramento Daily *Union*, 10/1/1864)

Of his visit to the places in the area of the new discoveries in and around Nevada, Browne wrote several "letters" that were published in the San Francisco *Bulletin* in late 1864 and early 1865. Letter No. 18 discussed the "Agricultural and Mineral Resources of East Walker River Valley." He detailed his trip to that locality, having departed the town of Aurora via the Elbow Ranch, where he "followed the right branch of the road across a desert valley, some eight miles in width, to a range of low mountains which intervenes between this point and Walker Valley..." Browne had taken the road that led east and northerly from Elbow Ranch and followed the line of the river. The "left branch" of the road would have taken him toward Sweetwater and on to Wellington's Station.

A portion of this letter discussed the "Gold Hill Range," of which, in part, he wrote:

"Attention was attracted to this range in 1861-2, and many enterprising adventurers from Esmeralda visited it with a view of opening the veins and working the ores. The outcroppings may be seen from the river, from which the principal system of leads is distant something over a mile. More than fifty claims were located, and several veins were opened with great promise of success. The average ores, as taken out, assayed from $50 to $100 to the ton. Professor Durant, of Oakland, was attracted thither by the excitement, and upon examination of the leads was so well satisfied of their value and permanence, that he built a mill for the purpose of reducing the ores. Owing to want of practical familiarity with the business and other causes, he made but one run, which, however, yielded $600, or at the rate of $20 to the ton. It was found that most of the gold had passed through the mill and that the tailings were the best part of the results. The machinery was clumsy and defective, and it became evident that additional expense must be incurred before the enterprise could be made profitable.

At this period, a great flood swept the valley. All industry was at an end for the time. This was in the winter of 1862, known as the great season of floods... Professor Durant lost all he had invested in the mill. In the meantime, public attention was attracted to other discoveries, and thus the Gold Range was temporarily abandoned...." (San Francisco *Bulletin*, 1/25/1865)

A correspondent of the San Francisco *Bulletin* wrote in early September, 1865, about his trip from California to Ione, in Nye County, east of Esmeralda County, writing about places he passed, and "The Mines on the Way":

"About ten miles to the east of the east fork of Walker river and to the south of the Wellington [toll] road is a range of metaliferous country stretching for 15 or 20 miles along the west base of the mountains that separate this stream from

Walker's lake. Here as much as four years ago were taken up a good many ledges for the gold and silver they were supposed to contain, some of the prospecting well in these metals on the surface. So encouraging was the prospect then considered that several districts were formed on the belt of country lying between the river and the mountains, some of the ledges located being quite out upon the plains, and a considerable amount of work done. The Rev. Henry Durand [sic], then essaying the miner's calling by way of repairing his health, thought so favorably of these mines that, aided by others, he soon after erected a small quartz mill on the river, several arastras being mean time put up by others. Having no facilities for roasting or otherwise properly treating the ores, this mill did not meet with much success; and having since been burnt down, there is now no kind of reduction works in that section of country, nor, until recently, has much since that period been attempted towards developing the mines. Within the past year what are thought to be rich lodes of copper ore have been found in that vicinity, upon a few of which work is now going on..." (San Francisco *Bulletin*, 9/7/1865)

In 1865, J. Ross Browne's account of his 1864 trip to "The Walker River Country," in *Harper's* magazine, included the following extracted information:

"One of the notable features of the country is the Gold Hill Range, situated about two miles from Shimmen's Ranch. Some very promising auriferous veins were discovered here in 1862, and there was, as usual, a great rush to the Walker River country...

A worthy Professor of my acquaintance living in Oakland was attracted thither by the noise of the discovery. It was his ambition to make a fortune, and devote the remainder of his days to the study of Plato and Aristotle. He knew nothing about quartz-mines or quartz-mills; but he was a classical scholar and a gentleman of varied scientific attainments. Of what avail was all this knowledge if he could not build a quartz-mill? He was poor, but he had friends and credit. Like a brave man he went to work, and by dint of algebraic equations, trigonometry, geometry, and an occasional reference

140

to Plato and Aristotle, he built a quartz-mill. On the banks of Walker River the wreck of that mill stands to this day. I saw it myself, and made a sketch of it from the Granite Bluff.

I refer to this mill as a solemn warning to Professors. There was no trouble about getting the ores. Wagon-loads came pouring down from the Gold Hill Range. The Professor was in ecstasies. His mill-wheels flew around with a tremendous clatter; his battery battered up the quartz at an amazing rate; his amalgamating pans made the finest suds! All went ahead smashingly – only the machinery was new and required grease. The Professor greased it – greased the water-wheel, the battery, the amalgamating pans, every thing that was worried by friction. Then the machinery worked to a charm; then the Professor gazed admiringly and was pleased to think that he would soon be able to retire into the quiet shades of his Academical groves. Well, the Professor is a kind friend and a good neighbor. I must deal gently with him.

When the great day came to determine the result of all this working – to test the wonderful advantages of education and intellect over vulgar prejudice in matters of this kind – the wheels were stopped, the pans were cleaned up, and the result was – I would be sorry to hazard a conjecture where it was. People said it was in the tailings. Back of the mill was a sluice which was found to be rich in gold. At all events the gold was nowhere else. Some hinted that grease and quartz have no amalgamating affinities, that the grease carried the precious metals with it; but this I consider a thoughtless fling at the Professor. The trouble was in the machinery.

A few thousand dollars would remedy it. But thousands of dollars were getting scarce.

Then came the disastrous flood of '62. It swept down the valley from the gulches and canons of the Sierra Nevadas, carrying with it haystacks, cabins, and even farms. I knew a man whose entire farm was swept clean off – soil, house, barns, haystacks, fences and all. There was nothing left of it but a desert sand-bottom. The honest miners were nearly starved out. The roads to Aurora and Carson were cut off by impassable torrents and lagoons. There was no such thing as travel, except on the rugged ridges of the mountains. The Professor was forced to abandon his mill and seek refuge in a hole which he and his friends burrowed in a neighboring hill. Here a happy coterie of hardy adventurers lay blockaded nearly all the winter. Sometimes the Professor read his beloved Plato, or philosophized to his fellows like Diogenes in his tub; sometimes he looked out upon the dreary expanse of water, and saw with sorrow his mill and his hopes of the Academical groves vanish day by day. Spring came at last; the country dried up; the Professor cast a long lingering look at the wreck of his mill, girded up his loins, and with a heavy sigh wended his way homeward, serious but not subdued. He is still an enthusiastic believer in that mill and the Walker River country..." (J. Ross Browne, *Harper's New Monthly Magazine*, Vol. 31, Issue 186, November 1865)

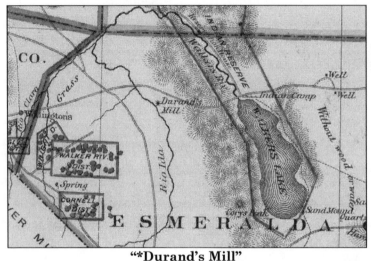

"*Durand's Mill"
(Map of the Public Lands of Nevada; General Land Office, 1866)

The use of the asterisk (*) with the name of the mill site, likely was to indicate that the mill was no longer functional at the time of the publication of this U.S. Government map. This General Land Office map (shown on pg. 147) was probably the last to show the location of Durant's mill site. The map shows the river by the name of "Rio Ida," instead of "East Walker River."

In a report from Jas. H. Smith, Esmeralda County Assessor, Smith advised the State of the number of ore crushing mills located in the county. In regard to the area of the East Walker River, Smith reported that there was "One three-stamp mill, worked by water power on the East Walker River." (*Journal of the Senate, Second Session of the Legislature of the State of Nevada*, 1866; Appendix to Report of Surveyor General; Reports of County Surveyors and County Assessors, p. 42) **This may have been Durant's Mill.**

Rev. Henry Durant

Browne's account confirms that the flooding written of by the Aurora correspondent had indeed devastated the mills that had been erected on the river. However, although Browne's comment that the "Professor" was forlorn about this loss, it may be noted that the man of whom he wrote, was Rev. Henry Durant, not Durand, and that, while he may have been disappointed by the loss and lack of success with the mill, he probably did not return home a devastated man.

Rev. Henry Durant

Durant was the founder of the Oakland College School, in 1855, which later became the University of California, at Berkeley. He was well connected in society and highly respected by most that associated with him.

Fifty-one year old Henry Durant was a Congregational minister who left Massachusetts in 1852 for California. Going to Nevada City, he opened a school there. Durant later returned to the bay area, where he founded the College School, at Oakland, serving as both a professor and a trustee.

An account of Mr. Durant's life published on the UC Berkeley's website, notes much of his history in an interesting chronology that illuminates the importance of the Professor's contribution to education in the golden state. As regards the time period of which we know Durant was in Nevada, the website's history includes this:

> "Money was still needed for its [the college] upkeep; it has been reported that Durant was so devoted to his college work that in 1861-1862, while nearing sixty years in age, he worked in a mine in the Sierras to gain money for its development, but not with notable success. More than likely, this was a promotional venture, one which required and involved no real labor."

Obviously the historian who wrote the above passage had little knowledge of mining or milling operations or else would have known that the aging Professor likely worked dawn to dusk to get his mill up and running, all the while keeping accurate records for the investors of the S. F. Trust and Mining Company, which was undoubtedly formed to finance the endeavor. Durant was acquainted with many of the big names in the Oakland and San Francisco area, some of whom also served as trustees on the College's board.

Mineral City

Massachusetts-born Edwin A. Sherman, was a California pioneer and Mexican War veteran, who was the editor and publisher of the Aurora *Star* newspaper from 1862 to 1864, in the new town of Aurora. He was also a surveyor by trade, according to the 1860 census of Los Angeles County.

In or about August of 1864, Mr. Sherman set out to survey a new town in the county of Esmeralda that was named "Mineral City." Comprised of some 165 (proposed) town blocks, like Granite City before it, Mineral City was planned to be located at the site of Durant's Mill.

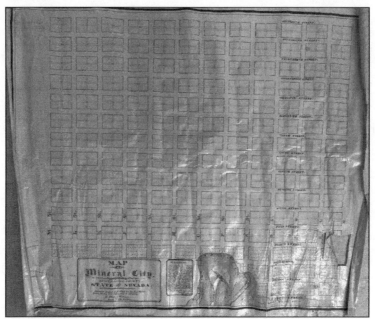

← North (Full Map) → South

144

**Map of Mineral City, Esmeralda County, State of Nevada
Surveyed August A.D. 1864 For the East Walker River Mining
and Agricultural Company**
(Edwin A. Sherman, Deputy County Surveyor, August 1864; North is at left)

The text in the Description shown above, states:

> "Mineral City lies about 35 miles in a northerly direction from Aurora. It is laid out in accordance with the late Act of Congress, and is situated on the Eastern side of the East Walker River, and as near the center of the East Walker River Mining District as could be estimated.
>
> The town site is divided into 165 Blocks, with 16 lots in each block excepting the fractional blocks Nos. 4, 5, 6, 14, & 15.
>
> The Streets run due north and South and due East and West, and are 80 feet in width. The alleys are 20 feet wide and intersect each other in the center of the blocks. The lots are 42 feet wide and 100 feet in depth, containing 4,200 square feet. The blocks, measuring from street to street, east and west are 220 feet, from North to South are 356 feet.
>
> The lot stakes west of Fourth Street have all be driving, East of it they soon will be driven.
>
> Area of Town Site 640 Acres.
>
> August 1864
>
> Edwin A. Sherman
>
> Deputy Co. Surv."

In mid-October 1864, the Sacramento Daily *Union* wrote an item titled, "For Plymouth Rock," which noted:

"We were yesterday shown by E. A. Sherman, of Aurora, a piece of rock, weighing five pounds, taken from the Young America lead, which is being sent by the Lincoln and Johnson Club, of Aurora, to New England to be exchanged for a piece of Plymouth Rock... He goes East as the agent of the East Walker River Mining and Agricultural Company – a company by which Mineral City has been laid out on the East Walker, and a large amount of mineral ground located." (Sacramento Daily *Union*, 10/13/1864)

In his letter to the San Francisco *Bulletin*, in January 1865, J. Ross Browne also wrote of "Mineral City." On his tour of the "East Walker River Valley," Browne had described the places he reached along the road from Elbow Ranch. Of Mineral City, Browne reported:

"A site has also been chosen for a town, located on the banks of the river, at a point overlooking the whole country. The plan, as surveyed by Major Sherman, is well adapted to the local peculiarities of the place. "Mineral City" – the proposed name of the town – has a water front of a mile or more, and lies about midway between the northern and southern extremities of the valley. For convenience of access and security against Indian hostilities, the position is the best that could be selected; although there are other points on the river which will doubtless became valuable for town sites as soon as the valley is rendered available for settlement on a large scale by the proposed irrigation system. I should mention that most of the bottom lands, bordering immediately on the river, are now under cultivation by settlers who have stopped here during the past two years. There must now be some eight or ten farms on the river..." (San Francisco *Bulletin*, 1/25/1865)

E. A. Sherman was also mentioned in J. Ross Browne's 1865 article on "The Walker River Country," in *Harper's New Monthly Magazine*, in which Browne wrote:

"A few farms had been started on the bottom lands, and we passed some very cozy little farmhouses and thrifty gardens. The river is fringed with willow, sycamore, and a species of cotton-wood, resembling balm of Gilead. We followed its course about seven miles through a series of narrow valleys, on the left side, till we reached a gorge in the mountains through which it passes. At this point there is a good ford, over which we crossed. Lawson's Ranch commences here. A drive of half a mile took us to the house; a frame shanty pleasantly situated near the road. Mr. Lawson was at home, and kindly offered us the accommodations of his place...

Lawson's Ranch may be considered the beginning of the main East Walker River Valley. The bottom gradually widens. On the right lies a sloping plain, barren in appearance but abounding in some of the finest lands east of the Sierras. A survey of this country has recently been made by Major E. A. Sherman, under the auspices of a company of Aurorians, with a view of opening it up for settlement. It is in contemplation to make a canal or acequia from Lawson's Ford for the purpose of irrigating the extensive tract of land now lying waste between the foot-hills and the river bottom..."

It is almost certain that the "extensive tract of land," of which J. Ross Browne wrote that Sherman was involved, was that area of the proposed town of Mineral City, although at the time of the magazine's article Browne had perhaps found it necessary to delete a reference to it, in that the plans for the town site never fully materialized.

Indeed, the town site venture for Mineral City did not take wings or fly. There is seemingly no official record of the town site plat of Mineral City presently available anywhere in Nevada.

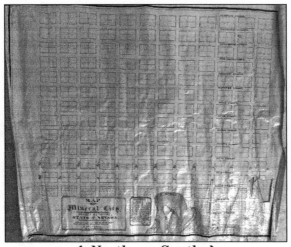

← North ~ South →

147

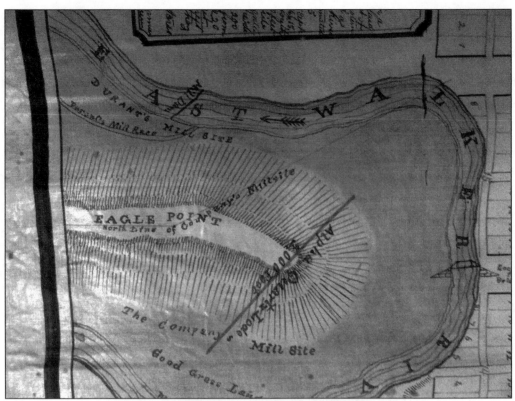

Durant's Mill Race, Durant's Mill Site and
"The Company's Mill Site" on "Eagle Point"
(River shown to the right is East →)

Wheeler Ranch

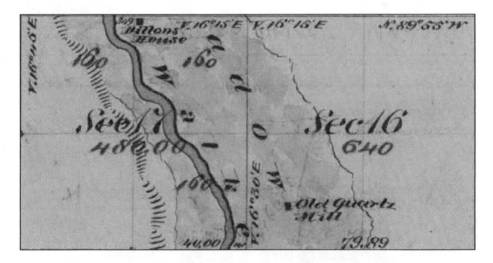

One key to a potential site for the location of Durant's Mill might be found in the General Land Office Rectangular Survey map issued in

1869 for Township 10 North, Range 27 East. In this year, the government showed the location of an "Old Quartz Mill," in Section 16, approximately three miles north of the Shimmin Ranch.

In a letter to the Sacramento Daily *Union*, one correspondent wrote of an incident of flooding in the vicinity of Aurora in late December, 1867. In this letter, the writer noted, "The last heard from John Wheeler's the water was four feet in and around the house." The article also noted that the East Walker was "five feet higher than ever before known." (Sacramento Daily *Union*, 1/11/1868)

In September of 1869, a correspondent wrote that, "John Wheeler is putting up a ten stamp mill near Pine Grove, to work the rock of his mine, which is said to be rich, and the mine a large one and well developed." (Sacramento Daily *Union*, 9/1869) By late October, the stamp mill was completed and about to begin running. (Sacramento Daily *Union*, 10/27/1869) The mill mentioned in the foregoing was erected on the eastern portion of Pine Grove, a little north of the Wheeler mine. It was **not** the mill shown in the above map view.

The survey field notes of the 1869 survey identified the house of John Wheeler, north and beyond the Shimmin Ranch, in T10N R27E. While surveying the line running north between sections 21 and 22, the surveyor noted that "John Wheelers house bears S 61° 20' W." The next line of the field notes has an erasure of what was initially written "Old man Wheelers," with a ditto mark (") for "house," which was replaced with just the word "House." The location of this "House," was reported to be located N 78° 40' W of the location on the north-south line between sections 21 and 22. The line after that identified the location of "Dick Wheelers house" at N 38° 11' W. The surveyor also noted that from the corner common to sections 16, 17, 20 and 21, the "furnace stack in old Quartz Mill bears N. 42.45 E distant 40.40 ch." (BLM Nevada Land Records, R0057, 5/19/1869)

It is not known if this "old quartz mill" represented the mill of Henry Durant or a later mill that may have been erected. In 1863, "Wheelers" was shown as being south of "Durand's Mills," per DeGroot's Map of Nevada Territory (see page 137), so it is certain that the Wheeler's were residing in the area at least that early.

Members of the family of John Wheeler and his Illinois-born wife, Martha (Patsy) Willis, were first found in Carson Valley, Utah

Territory on the 1860 census. These included father John Wheeler and son, Henry Wheeler, who were living together. Daughters Margaret Wheeler Mott, wife of Squire Mott of Mottsville history, and Docia (Martha D.) Wheeler, were living nearby, as was eldest son, Merrill W. Wheeler and his family. The remainder of the family, including sons Thomas J. Wheeler and John J. Wheeler and daughter Lucy Ann Wheeler were living at Salt Lake City, Utah Territory.

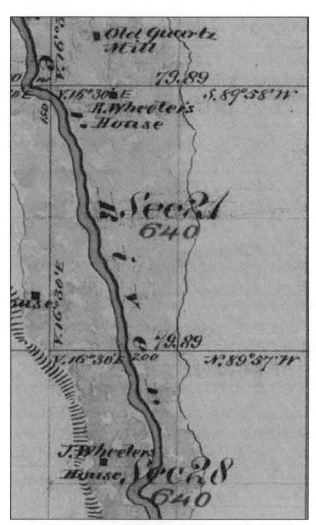

Quartz Mill, R. (Dick) Wheeler's and J. Wheeler's House
(General Land Office, T10N R27E, M. D. M., 1869)

According to the *First Directory of Nevada Territory*, H. C. (Henry) Wheeler was at Aurora, in the Esmeralda Mining District. Thomas Wheeler was listed in the directory as being at Empire City, east of Carson City. Thomas and one of his brothers, historically referred to as the "Wheeler Bros.," in some accounts, were later living on the West Fork of the Walker River, just south of its confluence with the East Walker River.

The Sacramento Daily *Union* reported in May, 1862, on a "Fatal Affray on East Walker River," writing:

> "A correspondent of the Union, writing from Johnson district, East Walker River, Nevada Territory, May 10th, relates the following: Daniel S. Toomey [sic], a native of Ireland, aged about forty-seven years, died in this camp yesterday from the effect of wounds received on Sunday, April 28th, at the hands of John Wheeler. The affray grew out of some harsh language indulged in by both parties at Wheeler's ranch, on West Walker river, a few days previous to the fight. At the time of the first dispute, they separated without blows.
>
> On Sunday, as above stated, Wheeler came to this camp and meeting Toomey [Toumey], an altercation followed, in the course of which Wheeler drew a navy size revolver and struck Toomey a number of blows on the head and arm, inflicting some severe gashes on the head, besides bruising his left arm so severely as partially to paralyze it. A physician from Aurora was called, who examined and probed the wounds on his head and pronounced the skull fractured in two or three places, one of them depressing the skull on his brain in such a manner as to produce inflammation, congestion and as a consequence, death.
>
> Toomey had a brother, whose name, in his partially conscious condition, he gave as Dennis S. Toomey, and who, when he last heard from him, was boarding at the Philadelphia House on Pacific or Washington streets, San Francisco. The brother of the deceased is a glass-blower by trade, and with this communication is sent to your journal with a request for publication, with the view that the brother of deceased may hear of the occurrence. By publishing the above, or the facts recited therein, you will confer a favor. Toomey left some few hundred dollars worth of property, which will be safely cared for. Wheeler has not yet been arrested."

In November of 1862, daughter Lucy Ann Wheeler was married to William Wallace, probably at Mottsville, in Douglas County, Nevada Territory. (Western States Marriages)

In a record left by Joseph I. Wilson, son of David Wilson of Pine Grove and Mason Valley history, Joseph noted that on "the first of September, 1863, my father, David Wilson, and my uncle, William Wilson, purchased squatters rights of the Wheeler family to approximately 4000 acres for the sum of $2,000..." (Reno Evening *Gazette*, 7/17/1954)

Wilson's account also contained the following, which includes the activities of the Wheeler's before and during the discovery at Pine Grove, Nevada:

> "'Pap' Wheeler and his seven sons had squatted on unsurveyed land under the Utah law in 1860. The land they chose was on the west fork of the Walker river, in the extreme southern end of Mason Valley. The Wheelers had erected earth boundary mounds, and three years were allowed them to fence and indicate their boundary lines...
>
> The Pioneer, the first quartz mill in Pine Grove, was built by the Wheeler Bros. Free milling for gold rock, it had 15 stamps, steam power, using wood for fuel...
>
> P. Manson was one doctor in Pine Grove in the boom days, while B. Mason was the other. The notary public was T. Abrams. The justice of the peace was Daniel (Dan) Wheeler....
>
> It was nearly 1/2 mile between the upper and the lower town (Pine Grove). The school and a scattering of houses were in that 1/2 mile stretch. The first school teacher was Miss Docia Wheeler, and the second was Mrs. Glann...
>
> The Wheeler mine was worked at a depth of 200 feet by 40 men and an estimated $2,000,000 was taken out. It was sold to Pope and Talbot for $50,000..."

In Thompson & West's *History of Nevada* (1881), it was noted that "Tom Wheeler and brother settled about eighteen miles south of (N. H. A.) Mason's Ranch, on the west fork of Walker River, in the fall of 1866. The place is now owned by D. Wilson..." In 1913, Sam P. Davis, in his history of Nevada, noted that following the 1860 erection of Mason's house (in Mason Valley), "were the Wheeler brothers, who settled on what is now a part of the George Wilson ranch." The differing dates aside, all accounts verify that the Wilson's acquired lands from the Wheeler family members.

The Wilson ranch was located on the east end of the canyon through which the West Walker River runs, known now as Wilson Canyon, at the extreme south end of Mason Valley. It was northwest from the lands settled by John Wheeler and his sons, shown on the 1869 map.

In early March, 1865, the Daily *Alta California* newspaper included a report that a "Mr. Wheeler arrived from the East Fork of the Walker River and reported that on the 28th of January, Wm. Stuart [sic] and a man named Dutch Bob had left Columbus mining district, which is some ninety miles southeast of Walker River, for their homes, on the east fork of that river, but not having arrived on the 17th of February, their neighbors suspected that they had been murdered by the Indians." (Daily *Alta California*, 3/3/1865)

Roughly ten days later the Sacramento Daily *Union* carried an item titled, "Indian Expedition from Fort Churchill," which advised that, "Tomorrow at daylight, a detachment of fifty men of Companies D and E, Nevada Cavalry, and 35 men of Company A, Nevada Infantry, under command of Captain William Wallace, will leave for Walker Lake..." (Sacramento Daily *Union*, 3/13/1865) The Army sought to identify and capture the Paiute Indians involved in the murder of Stewart and Rabe (the true name of "Dutch Bob").

Captain William Wallace was the son-in-law of Wheeler family patriarch John Wheeler, and the brother-in-law of Richard, Thomas, Henry and John J. Wheeler, all known to be living in the vicinity at the time.

In a report of the expedition filed by Wallace, he wrote, "Left Wilson's at five o'clock A. M. on the 14th, traveled fifteen miles, and camped on Wheeler's ranch, on the west side of the East Fork of Walker's river." The "Wilson's" mentioned by Wallace was likely the David and William Wilson ranch purchased in 1863 from the Wheeler family, as noted by Joseph I. Wilson in his historical notes published in 1954.

By 1868, Captain William Wallace was residing on Curry Street, in Carson City and was listed in the 1868-1869 Nevada Directory. That same year, Martha D. Wheeler, daughter of patriarch John Wheeler, was married to A. J. Smith, of Reno. In 1870, Mr. Smith was employed as a "Town Agent" by the Central Pacific Railroad Company, proponents of the founding of the city of Reno.

By the time of the 1870 census, members of the Wheeler family were living at various places around the State. Father John Wheeler and sons "Wesley" (William Wesley) and "Edward" (Daniel Edward) Wheeler were enumerated in Pine Grove Township, where they were farming, likely on the land shown on the General Land Office map of 1869. Son John J. Wheeler, his wife and two children were living at Aurora or nearby, where John was a miner. Daughter Martha D., her husband A. J. Smith and 11 month old daughter Millie were residing in Reno. Captain William Wallace, wife Lucy Ann and their four children were in Carson City.

While Richard (Dick) Wheeler had been mentioned in the surveyor's field notes for the 1869 General Land Office survey of T10N R27E, he was not found by census in either 1860 or 1870. In 1873, however, a letter from Aurora appeared in the Sacramento Daily *Union*, which reported that, "Richard Wheeler left here yesterday afternoon on horseback for Pine Grove, and when about five miles out, the girth of the saddle got loose, and the horse threw him, breaking his arm near the shoulder." Doctor and lawyer, David J. Lewis, of Aurora, was sent to provide medical service for the injured man. (Sacramento Daily *Union*, 5/31/1873)

In the 1875 Nevada State Census, W. W. Wheeler, a stock raiser, was enumerated a short distance north from the Shimmin Ranch. Brother Henry Wheeler lived at the C. J. Dunlap household and was a stock raiser. Thomas Wheeler, also a stock raiser, was residing in Washoe County, with his wife, the former Elizabeth "Lizzie" Perkins of Franktown, and their infant son, P. H. Wheeler.

The elusive Richard Wheeler, as he had previously been on earlier censuses, was missed by the State census lists in 1875, but word of him, however, was reported in October of 1875:

> "The Lyon County Times of the 5th says: A boy rode into Dayton yesterday morning from Mason Valley in hot haste for a doctor. He brings the report that one Pat Birmingham shot, and it is supposed, mortally wounded Mr. Richard Wheeler, on Sunday night at that place, and that after the shooting

Birmingham escaped. Wheeler is a brother-in-law of Judge Seawell, and holds the same relation to Constable Smith of Virginia City." (Daily *Alta California*, 10/7/1875)

Judge W. M. Seawell's wife was Susan A. Scrivner, sister of the wife of John J. Wheeler. Constable Smith was A. J. Smith, the husband of Martha D. Wheeler and son-in-law of patriarch John Wheeler.

John J. Wheeler went to Bodie, at the height of its boom between 1877 and 1880. In the former year, John worked as a teamster. He may have been the "black sheep" of the Wheeler family. Evidence of this is found from two incidents where he seemed to have run into at least two difficulties while at Bodie, as the following accounts attest:

John J. Wheeler (circa 1865)
(Courtesy of Terry Anderson)

"Pacific Coast News.

About a week ago at Bodie an American named John Wheeler had trouble with a Mexican, one Revis, which ended in the latter receiving his death wound. The particulars of the affair, as related to us, says the Carson *Tribune* of August 15, are as follows:

Some time since Revis secured a contract from the Standard Mining Company to furnish said company several thousand cords of wood. He sub-let a portion of the contract to Wheeler. The contract being finished, Revis applied and received payment for his wood in two or three large checks. He tendered one of them to Wheeler, who refused to receive it, stating that he wanted the coin. Revis said he could not settle in that way, when Wheeler jerked out his pistol, and remarking, "We'll settle it this way," fired three shots into the Mexican's body, killing him instantly. There must be another side of the story for, at a preliminary examination, Wheeler was discharged from custody..." (*Territorial Enterprise*, 8/16/1877)

"Pacific Coast News.

A shooting scrape without serious results happened at Bodie last Thursday between J. L. Blethen and John Wheeler. That man Wheeler seems to like such things. This is his third exercise of the kind within a few weeks." (*Territorial Enterprise*, 12/26/1877)

By 1881, John J. Wheeler, his father John Wheeler and brother William Wesley Wheeler were residing in Idaho. In the course of events, John J. Wheeler had a run in with Tom Miles in which Wheeler shot Miles and was arrested. He was released on $1,000 bail, which was ultimately forfeited when he failed to appear at trial. His father and brother surrendered the forfeited payment. (Idaho *Statesman*, 10/22/1881 and 7/20/1882)

John Joshua Wheeler
(Courtesy of Terry Anderson)

John J. Wheeler was later sent to Folsom State Prison, in California for a term of two years, after being tried for shooting a man named W. P. Gaby at the town of Fort Bidwell, in Modoc County. Convicted in August of 1883, he was received at the prison on August 18, 1883 to begin serving his sentence. The inmate register of the prison described that Wheeler had "Broad large features, (a) long scar on right side of neck, (a) black mark 1 in. from ear on neck, (also same) on back of neck (and a) scar on 1st joint of lft index finger."

As the result of a petition drive undertaken and signed by a vast number of residents, including the Modoc County Sheriff, on August 11th, 1884 California Governor George B. Stoneman pardoned Wheeler and he was released from prison on August 13th, having served just one year of his term. (Modoc County Superior Court docket, Case No. 634, Folsom Prison Inmate Register and Petition to Governor Stoneman, dated March 1884, courtesy of Terry Anderson, Wheeler descendant)

Richard Wheeler, it seems, was not killed by Pat Birmingham in 1875, for in 1878 he was mentioned in a news item quoting information from his brother-in-law, A. J. Smith. Smith stated that:

"At Grant Mountain Hank Blanchard and Dick Wheeler and others have a mine, the ore of which yields by mill process $80 per ton in gold and silver. They have six men at work, and are confident that they will soon develop a very valuable mine." (*Territorial Enterprise*, 1/6/1878)

Given the location of "R. Wheeler's house" in 1869 and knowing that he was working a mine on Mount Grant, it is very likely that Wheeler Pass was named for Dick Wheeler or others of his family. This pass connects to the present-day road that leads to the Cottonwood Creek Road, west and above the town of Walker Lake that leads southerly toward Lapon Meadows at the head of Lapon Canyon. This pass undoubtedly saved Wheeler many miles of travel.

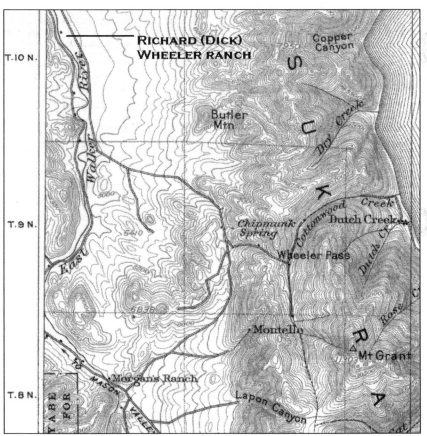

Wheeler Ranch and Wheeler Pass (right center above)
(USGS Hawthorne Quadrangle, 1909)

From a news article out of Yerington in 1909, improvements to Wheeler Pass were noted:

"...Continued activity is apparent in the Mount Grant district at the southern end of the Mason valley. The new road through Wheeler pass to the Gold Note will be completed this week, and Manager Vance of the Gold Note says that upon its completion an automobile will be able to cross the range with ease. The opening of the pass to other means of transportation besides horseback will result in a number of properties opening up this coming spring, and with the melting of the winter snows the road will be dotted with ore teams hauling their freight to the mills." (Los Angeles *Herald*, 11/30/1909)

In 1880, most of the Wheeler family members were located as they had been in 1875. The exceptions to this were William and Lucy Ann Wallace, who had moved to Lake City, in Modoc County, California; and John Wheeler's wife, Fannie, who, with the Wheeler children, had gone to San Joaquin County to reside with her parents, Benjamin and Talitha Scrivner. By 1883, John Wheeler and family were also living at Lake City, Modoc County.

Despite the fact that the Wheeler "houses" along the East Walker River had been shown on the 1869 Township map, it wasn't until 1884 that contract land patents were secured by son Henry Wheeler from the State of Nevada. The parcel, in which "J. Wheeler's house" had been shown, was purchased from the State by M. E. Bryant, in 1879.

Henry's lands were listed to be within sections 8, 16 and 17 of T10N R27E, including the Southwest quarter of the Southwest quarter of Section 16, in which the "Old Quartz Mill" was shown in 1869. The location of Richard Wheeler's house, in Section 21, was also included in the lands patented to Henry Wheeler.

Sad and tragic news faced the Wheeler and Wallace families in February of 1885, on the death of William Wallace, formerly the Commander of Fort Churchill, Nevada:

"Captain William Wallace Killed.
Lake City, Cal., Feb. 5.
    Editor Gazette – Last evening, while standing at the bar in the saloon at this place, Captain Wm. Wallace was fatally stabbed by W. B. King. The circumstances, as near as we could learn, were as follows:
    Wallace and King had been playing cards, and when they

158

had finished went up to the bar. They were in the act of drinking when King suddenly drew his knife and stabbed Wallace twice in the shoulder, and as he turned around he got a gash across his abdomen, extending about six inches. Not being satisfied with this he cut him twice more, once in the arm and once in the thigh. Wallace suffered the most intense agony until 6 o'clock this morning, when he died. King is under arrest at Cedarville. He is one of Surprise Valley's oldest settlers.

Captain Wallace formerly resided in Carson for several years. He was in the army during the war and D. H. Pine was his First Lieutenant. He was in charge at Fort Churchill awhile. He was an old resident of Douglas county and was married to a sister of Tom Wheeler's of Reno. He was a carpenter by trade and a very intelligent man and a good citizen. For some years he has been merchandising at Lake City, Cal., but is said to have failed recently." (Reno Evening *Gazette*, 2/9/1884)

William B. King pleaded guilty at trial and was sentenced to life in California's state prison. (Reno Evening *Gazette*, 5/2/1885) He left a wife and six children to provide for themselves.

Two years later, an interesting item appeared in the Reno Evening *Gazette*, titled "A Pioneer Pioneering It":

"John Wheeler, 88 years of age, with a double team, came into Reno last Sunday night from Weiser, Idaho, traveling alone over the mountains a distance of 600 miles. He returns within a few days in the same way. He was a soldier in the Black Hawk and Seminole wars, and thinks himself as young now as then when in the service of Uncle Sam. He is stopping here with his father-in-law [sic] A. J. Smith."

The fate of patriarch John Wheeler was learned in two small news items from Idaho, in November, 1899:

"Old Timer Gone – Found Dead in His Room in a Weiser Hotel
    Weiser, Nov. 14. – John Wheeler, an old-timer, was found dead in his room at the Weiser hotel Sunday. He lived for many years in Washington county, but had more recently been a resident of Pioneer." (Idaho *Statesman*, 11/15/1899)
"John Wheeler Dead.

John Wheeler, an old time miner of Idaho and Washington county, was found lying dead on the floor of his room at the Hotel Weiser last Sunday morning. Mr. Wheeler has spent the past three years at Pioneerville, in Boise Basin. He died of miner's consumption and was on his way up the country to his brother [sic] Dick's." (Weiser *Signal*, 11/16/1899)

A native of North Carolina, John Wheeler had been born in 1802, and had lived nearly a century, experiencing the wilderness of the West as none today ever will again. He pioneered in Illinois, Utah, Nevada and Idaho.

By 1900, only Thomas J. Wheeler remained a resident of Nevada, living at Reno with his family, including three additional sons, Forrest, Adrian and Grover Wheeler. The other Wheeler family members were found living in Modoc or Mendocino counties, California, and William W. Wheeler was residing in Washington County, Idaho.

In 1908, Thomas Wheeler accompanied Churchill County surveyor, T. K. Stewart, who had been commissioned by the Churchill County Commissioners to survey the boundary line between Churchill and Esmeralda counties. Stewart's survey was to determine in which county the boom town of Rawhide was located. Thomas Wheeler "of Reno," had "located the old Mason house and other points" for Stewart, as the "Mason house, which was built in 1861, was the point of beginning for the official survey made in 1881..." (Reno Evening *Gazette*, 3/6/1908)

Two years later the news of the death of Thomas Wheeler was announced:

"Death Claims T. J. Wheeler.
Was One of State's Pioneers and Lived Long in Reno.

Thomas Jefferson Wheeler, another of the state's pioneers was called by death at his home at 1134 East 4th street at five thirty o'clock last evening. He had been ill for some time and little hope for his recovery was held out.

Mr. Wheeler crossed the plains in '49. He was one of the few persons who survived the terrible Mt. Meadow massacre in Utah. Coming to Nevada he turned his attention to mining which occupation he followed for a good part of his life. He has been a resident of Reno ever since there has been a Reno. He was a native of Illinois, aged 78 years. A wife and three sons, Parley, Adrian and Grover, all residing in Reno survive him.

The remains have been placed in charge of Perkins and Gulling. Funeral announcement will be made later."

With the death of Thomas, the last original Wheeler family member's history in Nevada came to an end. Thomas' wife, Lizzie Perkins Wheeler later died in 1916. This pioneer couple is buried in the Hillside Cemetery, in Reno, resting quietly in unmarked graves. Also in unmarked graves lie the remains of at least two of their sons, Parley Huston Wheeler and Forrest Wheeler.

The history of the Wheeler and Wallace families touched areas of Douglas, Esmeralda (now Mineral and Lyon), Ormsby (now Carson) and Washoe counties, in Nevada. Those who moved into California also helped to write the histories of Modoc and Mendocino counties.

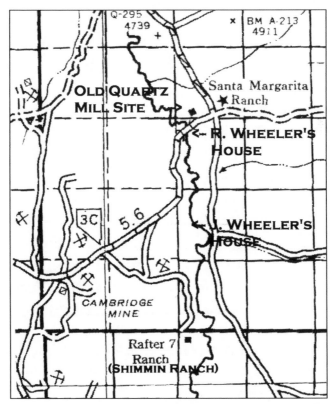

Location of Wheeler houses and Santa Margarita Ranch
(Nevada DOT Quad No. 1, 1968, annotated)

Santa Margarita Ranch

Today the old Wheeler ranch lands are a part of what is known as the Santa Margarita Ranch, north of the Rafter 7 Ranch.

From a brief review, it appears that the Wheeler ranch lands were later owned by Jules E. Gignoux (1847-1914), a mining engineer who came to Nevada around 1878. During his life in Nevada, A resident of Dayton, Gignoux served in the Nevada State Legislature; in the Assembly in 1881 and 1891 and in the Senate in 1893 and 1895, serving from Lyon County. Gignoux patented land north of the Wheeler's

In 1886, J. E. Gignoux's land, then in Esmeralda County, was valued at $3,425. By 1891, his holdings were valued at nearly $20,000. During the economic downturn of the 1890's, land values decreased across the board, but, by 1907, the Gignoux ranch on the East Walker River had an assessed value of nearly $12,000.

Mr. Gignoux died in March, 1914. On his death, the Regents of the University of Nevada passed a resolution in tribute to Gignoux, who was reported to have been the "first professor of mining and metallurgy in the university when it was at Elko..."

Gignoux's wife, May L. Gignoux, held the ranch property for only a short while after his death. In 1914, Mrs. Gignoux's real and personal property assessed in Mineral County, was valued at $20,594.

In March of 1910, J. E. Gignoux and his wife entered into a written contract with Ambro Rosaschi, to sell Rosaschi "certain lands in the County of Esmeralda, State of Nevada, for the sum of twenty-nine thousand dollars..." (J. J. Connelly Abstract Files; Estate of Efton Swindler) In 1912, the agreement to sell was converted to a mortgage held in the Farmers & Merchants National Bank, in which documentation records that the real property involved was "known as the Gignoux ranch, and the Mount Grant Range." (Mineral County Records, Volume 1 of Contracts, p. 60)

By 1917, the Wheeler ranch lands, in Mineral County, were owned by Ambro Rosaschi. According to tax assessment rolls, Mr. Rosaschi continued to own the property at least to 1930.

In 1900, Ambro Rosaschi (18 years, born Italy) and his brother, Romeo (20 years, born Italy), were enumerated as farm laborers working at

Lovelock, in Humboldt County, Nevada. Each brother stated they had arrived in the United States in 1898.

In 1910, Romeo Rosaschi was a farmer at Mason Valley and Ambro Rosaschi was enumerated in the Plummer precinct of Lyon County, with his wife of five years, Belle (20 years, born Nevada), and three children, Helen (3 years), Idele (2 years) and Ambro, Jr. (11 months), all born in Nevada. Mrs. Rosaschi was the former Belle McLeod, whom Mr. Rosaschi married June 15, 1905.

According to information included in an article about the Rosaschi's golden wedding anniversary, the couple resided "on a ranch near Yerington for six years, then on the old Gignoux ranch on East Walker River for 23 years...."

In 1914, Ambro Rosaschi of the "Haven Ranch, East Walker," became a charter member of the Nevada Cattle Owner's Association, an organization formed to address the business needs and requirements of Nevada stockmen.

Ten years later, Mr. Rosaschi ran afoul of the law:

> "Raises Headgate, Draws $50 Fine
> Yerington, Aug. 23 – (Special).
>
> Ambro Rosaschi, East Walker river rancher, was found guilty in the justice court at Hawthorne of tampering with the headgate of an irrigation canal which had been set by the water commission, and was fined $50 and costs.
>
> The defendant insisted he had a right to the water under a priority right granted in 1862, but the court held the water right was not the point at issue, but the interfering with the headgate, a misdemeanor under the state law.
>
> Justice of the Peace McCarthy granted a stay of execution for ten days in order to permit the defense to prepare an apeal [sic] to the district court." (Reno Evening *Gazette*, 8/23/1924)

In 1932, in a Notice of Judicial Sale that appeared in the Nevada State *Journal*, the District Court of the United States had issued an order of sale and decree of foreclosure in the matter of the Pacific National Agricultural Credit Corporation vs. Ambro Rosaschi and Belle Rosaschi, his wife, and Farmers Bank of Carson Valley, Inc., three "John Does" and three "Mary Roes," as defendants and Peter

Heitman, as a Cross Complainant and Intervenor in the matter. The property that was ordered sold was described as livestock "On 'Old Gignoux' or Rosaschi Ranch," in Mineral County, as well as livestock "On 'Old Campbell Ranch,'" in Lyon County. The notice gave no reason for the cause of action.

This same year, William M. Maule, Supervisor of the Mono National Forest, wrote in his diary notes that, having gone to Pine Grove, he went "down to Rosachi [sic] where (I) conferred with him relative to his last years payment." Rosaschi said it would be "settled pronto." Rosaschi's property, Maule wrote, "(is) now in the hands of (a) receiver" and it "looks abandoned; his cattle look fine however." (Maule, "Diaries of William M. Maule)

Rosaschi had either been foreclosed upon or had sold the old Wheeler and Gignoux ranches, moving to another location in the vicinity of Smith Valley. He became a prominent member of the Smith Valley community and remained on his Smith Valley ranch until his death in January of 1956. He was survived by his widow and thirteen of his surviving children. Ambro Rosaschi, Sr. was buried in St. Joseph's Catholic Cemetery adjacent to Valley View Cemetery, in Yerington.

Information on the ownership of the old Wheeler ranch after Ambro Rosaschi sold it has not been fully developed. From an old title abstract performed in 1939 by J. J. Connelly, then Mineral County Recorder at Hawthorne, Connelly reported that various lands, including those of the earlier Wheeler and Gignoux ranches, had been acquired by Peter and Louise Heitman, but transferred in 1935 to their children, William W. Heitman and Ida Theis. This would explain the reason why Heitman had intervened in the foreclosure suit again the Rosaschi's in 1932.

Some of the lands mentioned by Connelly were in Mineral County, located on the west slope of Mount Grant, while the East Walker ranch lands were then in Lyon County. The Mineral County lands held by Heitman and Theis were condemned under eminent domain for use by the Military Reservation for the Naval Ammunition Depot, at Hawthorne. (Reno Evening *Gazette*, 6/1/1939)

The Mason Valley Civilian Conservation Camp (CCC) hosted a tour of the many projects undertaken in the area by the men of Camp

Mason Valley. Among the places mentioned were the "Wheeler Flat dam" and the "Webster Summit drift fence." Among the ranchers invited to attend were Lafe Vannoy and Abe Charlebois. (Nevada State *Journal*, 4/6/1941) Vannoy owned the "Bar-A ranch on East Walker." (Reno Evening *Gazette*, 6/2/1939)

In 1945, a notation regarding the sale of livestock from the Nevada Hereford ranch, reported a prize bull had been "sold to William Rowe, of the Santa Margarita ranch, Yerington, for $2,000." (Reno *Gazette*, 2/26/1945) In May of 1951 it was reported that the "Rowe ranches which comprise the old Charlebois, Vannoy and Rosaschi ranches has been sold to Charles Fryer of the Fryer Cattle Company of San Francisco." The holdings included 4,000 acres of pasture and alfalfa land and 160,000 acres of range land. (Nevada State *Journal*, 5/4/1951) In 1953, Charles M. Fryer Cattle Company was reported to have sold the "Santa Margarita Ranch to Mr. and Mrs. Nate Wallace of Reno…" (Reno Evening *Gazette*, 8/19/1953) Wallace owned the property until 1967.

Thereafter, the following parties are named as potential owners or operators of the ranch: Oscar Ivey (1968-1970 and 1973-1976); Ivey Ranches (1977-1981); John Ivey (1982-1985); Cutler Ranch (1986-1988), and East Walker (1989-1995). (Walker River Basin Irrigation Diversions, Summary of Historic Surface Water Irrigation Diversions; Appendix B., Table B-7, p. 4; Randy Pahl, P.E., 2000)

Site of Durant's Mill Today

All of the ranches mentioned in this chapter have one thing in common – they were all near to or in the vicinity of Durant's Mill.

One of the keys to locating the site of Durant's Mill using current map and aerial photography, is held within the 1864 map of Mineral City. Edwin A. Sherman showed the location of Durant's Mill Site and "The Company's Mill Site" as being on "Eagle Point."

Sherman depicted Eagle Point as being a low hill range that jutted easterly to the west bank of the East Walker River. Mineral City was laid out on the alluvial plain to the east of the river. The following view shows a similar situated low hill range.

If the low hill range, at center in following aerial and topographic views, is that which Sherman called "Eagle Point," perhaps one day it may be verified as the site where Durant's mill was erected in 1861.

As one of the earliest known places along the East Walker River, confirmation of its location would add greatly to the knowledge of the early activities along the banks of this once wild river.

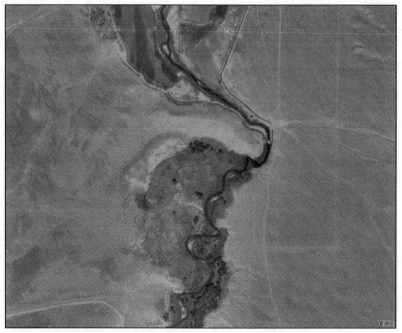

Possible site of "Eagle Point" and Durant's Mill
(USGS Butler Mtn Aerial, 8/19/2000)

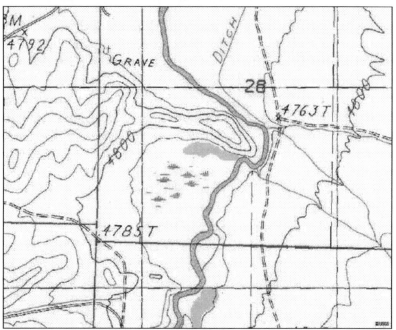

Possible "Eagle Point" site, in Sec. 28, T10N R27E, M.D.M.
(USGS Butler Mtn Quad, 7/1/1988)

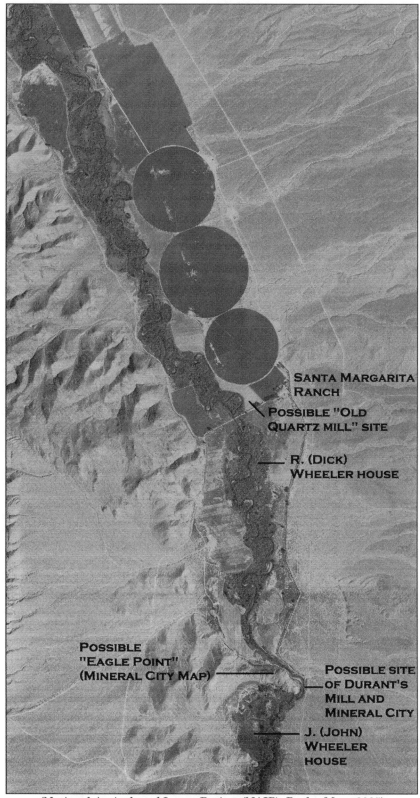

SANTA MARGARITA
RANCH

POSSIBLE "OLD
QUARTZ MILL" SITE

R. (DICK)
WHEELER HOUSE

POSSIBLE
"EAGLE POINT"
(MINERAL CITY MAP)

POSSIBLE SITE
OF DURANT'S
MILL AND
MINERAL CITY

J. (JOHN)
WHEELER
HOUSE

(National Agricultural Image Project (NAIP), Butler Mtn., 2005)

Spring runoff along the East Walker River
(Courtesy of Georgana Mayne)

Supplement

ROSS BROWNE'S LETTER – No. 18
Agricultural and Mineral Resources of East Walker River Valley
(San Francisco Bulletin, January 25, 1865; Extract)

Road From Aurora.

In the course of a tour through Nevada during the past summer, I had occasion to visit the country bordering on the eastern branch of Walker river. My principal object was to ascertain the agricultural and mineral resources of those out-of-the-way districts of which we had previously received but vague and indefinite accounts, and to embrace in these cursory sketches such information as would be likely to lead to further development of the country. Recent discoveries of coal and iron in the vicinity of Walker river induced me to extend my tour in that direction; and I now give you, according to promise, a brief synopsis of my observations.

An excellent grade, about five miles in length, extends from the town of Aurora to the head of an extensive sage desert, through which runs the main road to Carson City. A stunted and scraggy growth of pines, such as abounds on most of the spurs of the eastern slope, relieves in some degree the sterility of the mountains; but the forbidding aspect of the country is compensated by the wonderful variety and rich colors of the mineral strata abounding in every direction along the wayside.

At the **Five Mile House**, the first traveling station beyond Aurora, I saw something of the effects of cultivation as applied to the sage deserts. It is difficult to imagine a blade of grass could grow in such a barren-looking region; yet by the introduction of a small stream of water from a neighboring hill, and a very primitive system of irrigation, the owner of this station has redeemed a considerable tract of land and caused it to flourish with a luxuriant growth of cereals and vegetables. A more thrifty little farm could scarcely be found on the Western slope. The richness of the soil, apparently so barren, I had frequently observed in other parts of Nevada. Even in the neighborhood of Virginia City, wherever the earth is irrigated, it will produce abundant crops of vegetables. This convinces me that vast tracts of land in Nevada, now utterly worthless, could be made valuable by irrigation.

The Elbow.

Four miles further on, is another oasis in the desert where the road branches – one leading to Carson and the other to East Walker. The "Elbow"

169

is one of the numerous stopping-places which have grown up along the public highways within the past few years. A good and substantial house has been erected for the accommodation of travelers; whisky flows inside and running water outside, so that man or beast can be accommodated.

Road to Walker.

From the Elbow, I followed the right branch of the road across a desert valley, some eight miles in width, to a range of low mountains which intervenes between this point and Walker Valley. There is a natural pass in this range, through which the road winds for a distance of five miles. Although my wagon was heavily laden, I experienced no difficulty at any point in making the trip. By diverging a few miles to the right, a much shorter route to Walker Valley could be made; the only obstacles at present being some two or three ragged arroyas [sic], which would require bridging.

The Five-mile Cañon.

In passing through the cañon, the scenery is singularly wild and desolate, but possesses a rugged grandeur characteristic of most of the spurs of the Sierras. It would seem that Nature must have had a very lively time of it in many parts of this country; ripping up, tossing over, doubling under, and twisting asunder the crust of the earth. To the right can be seen at occasional intervals the towering peak of **Mount Grant** – so named in honor of our distinguished Federal General, by **Major E. A. Sherman**, who has recently made a topographical survey of this region. The usual scrubby growth of pine abounds in considerable quantities along the rugged declivities of the cañon. Strange and highly-colored outcroppings of minerals are everywhere perceptible. To my unlearned eye, it looked like a country in which vast treasures of gold and silver might be hidden for centuries without a chance of discovery; so vast, so rugged and irregular is the area of country over which the desolating convulsions wrought by flood and fire have extended in by-gone ages. If the precious ores do not exist in it, I am utterly at a loss to know for what purpose such a wierd [sic] blasted, fire-smitten country was created. Surely Nature in her benevolent system of compensations must have designed it for the practical uses of man rather than for the pleasure of the eye. Amid rocks and deserts that apparently forbid his approach, there is still an anomalous regard to his convenience. Roads are cut through mountains, in the form of natural passes, so systematically walled and graded, that one would suppose they had been made by contract, though it would require a stretch of the imagination to conceive that Government contractors had anything to do with them.

Descending the cañon at a gradual inclination, its walls converge till thy form a winding pass almost perpendicular on each side. Through this runs a narrow roadway, evidently the bed of a mountain stream, now quite dry and covered with fine gravel. I was told by my guides that excellent placer diggings had been discovered in this vicinity. The scarcity of water was the great obstacle to success.

Passing out of the cañon, a fine view is had of the Two Sentinels, **Mount Bullion** and **Mount Grant**, and of the rolling hills embraced within the intervening range of country in which important discoveries of coal have recently been made.

Coal Mines.

It may be well to mention in this connection that some days later I made a tour of the coal district. Several of the veins which I examined present evidence of coal deposits, some of them being as clearly defined as any I had previously seen in Puget's Sound. The excavations so far made have reached only the superficial strata, which is highly promising. The coal is a light carob, interline clear with shale and highly inflammable. Further explorations and experiments may result in the discovery of vast deposits of coal in this neighborhood. The surface of the earth for a distance of ten miles north and south, is speckled at intervals with glittering sheets of "shale," which experienced miners pronounce an infallible sign of the proximity of coal.

The importance of this discovery in a State like Nevada, where wood is scarce, and where the operations of mining require extraordinary supplies of fuel, cannot be too highly estimated. A few coal mines capable of supplying the mills of Washoe and Esmeralda, to say nothing of less noted Districts, would greatly lessen the cost of reducing the ores, and probably contribute more to the general prosperity of the country than any one product of the earth that could be named. The cost of transportation across the sierras precludes the supply of coal from California. Wood is constantly diminishing in quantity and becoming more difficult of access. It is a matter of vital interest, therefore, to the people of Nevada that these coal veins should be thoroughly explored.

Settlements on Walker River.

Leaving the coal-fields to the right, we skirted along the base of a mountain range to the left, till the road struck into the first series of small valleys lying along the course of the Walker river. The distance from Aurora to the first crossing of the river, I estimated to be about 25 miles. Several thrifty little farms are located in this vicinity. I conversed with the settlers along the way and found them very sanguine as to the future destiny of the

Walker river county. Their crops were abundant; their stock in good condition; and nothing seemed to trouble them save the encroachment of drovers from California, who had driven over their horses and cattle during the late drought, to seek a better range on the banks of the Walker.

Immigrant Trains.

As we passed down the valley on the left bank of the river, we encountered several immigrant trains, comprising a number of families and a good supply of stock, bound for California as soon as the pasture ranges on the other side would permit of their moving. They had been recruiting here for the past two months after their tedious journey across the plains. Some of them seemed disposed to stay, and establish farms on the river.

Walker River.

Even at this season of drought, the most severe ever known either in California or Nevada, the river contained an abundance of water. Draining as it does a vast area of the Sierra Nevadas, the source of supply is inexhaustible, and nothing can be purer than the water, which bounds in crystal clearness over the rocks. Groves of willow fringe the banks, interspersed here and there with some fine specimens of the balm of gilead [sic], and occasionally a group of sycamores.

Following its course through the first series of valleys, we crossed once more at **Lawson's ford**, where the mountains converge from each side, forming a kind of pass. Within a half mile of the crossing we came to **Lawson's ranch** – the first point of settlement at the head of the great valley. The rich alluvial river bottom gradually spreads from this point, till it assumes an average width of about a mile, embracing within its limits some excellent pasture lands. There is also a considerable portion of this bottom admirably adapted to farming purposes – especially to the growth of corn, pumpkins, melons, beets and such other products as require a light porous soil, with abundant moisture. On the right, beyond the margin of the bottom, (which is distinctly marked by willow bushes and a luxuriant growth of grass and weeds,) lies a broad, sloping plain, barren in appearance, but abounding in rich deposits of soil from the mountains.

The lands, I think, are better adapted to agricultural purposes than those in the low bottoms immediately on the banks of the river. The soil is rich and warm, but of course unproductive now for want of water. I understand it to be the design of a company of capitalists to open an acequia, or small canal, from the river, at some point in the neighborhood of Lawson's ranch, and run it down the valley on the inner circle of the foot hills; thus bringing the entire tract within the means of irrigation. There can be no doubt as to the feasibility of the plan. The cost would be but trifling, for Nature seems to have done the principal part of the work. The descent of the river is rapid, the volume of water inexhaustible; no obstacles of any kind intervene, the slope of the valley, both laterally and longitudinally, is just sufficient for successful irrigation, and the ground is easily worked. Probably a hundred thousand acres of rich arable land could thus be redeemed. The Spaniards in Sonora and Arizona have long since tested this question of irrigation. A large portion of Arizona, now a worthless desert, was successfully cultivated by means of acequias, during the existence of the Spanish missions; and the same is the case in Sonora.

Value of Agricultural Products in Nevada.

In a country where the area of agricultural lands is small – as is peculiarly the case in Nevada – the importance of an enterprise like this can scarcely be measured by its direct pecuniary results...

A ready market exists at Aurora, Genoa, Carson, Virginia City and Reese river, for all the products that could be raised here. The distance to Austin is about 120 miles; to Virginia City about the same; and to Aurora is about 35 miles, with good roads and no intervening mountains of any consequence. At present all the fruits and most of the grain used in Nevada are hauled across the Sierras from California. The cost of freight is from three to five cents a pound. This added to the original cost and necessary proat[?], renders the price of all such products in Nevada extravagantly high. It will thus bee seen that agricultural lands in any convenient location derive an extraordinary value from the proximity of the mines, and the ready market afforded by the demands of a large population engaged in speculative pursuits. Grain of all kinds could therefore be grown in this valley at an advantage over the imported article of the cost of transportation from California, which under the most favorable circumstances can never be less than the three cents a pound.

Mineral City.

A site has also been chosen for a town, located on the banks of the river, at a point of rocks overlooking the whole country. The plan, as surveyed by **Major Sherman**, is well adapted to the local peculiarities of the place. "Mineral City" – the proposed name of the town – has a water front of a mile or more, and lies about midway between the northern and southern extremities of the valley. For convenience of access and security against Indian hostilities, the position is the best that could be selected; although there are other points on the river which will doubtless become valuable for town sites as soon as the valley is rendered available for settlement on a

173

large scale by the proposed system of irrigation. I should mention that most are now under cultivation by settlers who have stopped here during the past two years. There must now be some eight or ten farms on the river.

Shimmen's Ranch.

During my stay in the vicinity of Lookout Mountain, a point about two miles above **Mineral City**, I was hospitably entertained at the residence of a Mr. Shimmens [sic], who has an excellent farm under cultivation. Within two years he has surrounded himself with most of the comforts of a civilized house. His pasture lands yield an abundance of hay; his fields teem with grain; his garden is stocked with the finest vegetables; and his cattle look as if they never lacked food. I have rarely enjoyed a better meal than I ate at his hospitable board; and little as it was to be expected, I found here evidence of refinement which would do credit to much older communities, such as books, musical instruments, etc.

Gold Hill Range.

Accompanied by Mr. Shimmens, Dr. Manning and some other gentlemen who felt a great interest in the development of this country, I took an early opportunity to visit the celebrated "Gold Hill Range" – so called from the number of auriferous veins discovered here a few years ago. Attention was attracted to this range in 1861-62, and many enterprising adventurers from Esmeralda visited it with a view of opening the veins and working the ores. The outcroppings may be seen from the river, from which the principal system of leads is distant something over a mile. More than fifty claims were located, and several veins were opened with great promise of success. The average ores, as taken out, assayed from $50 to $100 to the ton. **Professor Durant**, of Oakland was attracted thither by the excitement, and upon examination of the leads was so well satisfied of their value and permanence, that he built a mill for the purpose of reducing the ores. Owing to want of practical familiarity with the business and other causes, he made but one run, which, however, yielded $600, or at the rate of $30 to the ton. It was found that most of the gold had passed through the mill and that the tailings were the best part of the results. The machinery was clumsy and defective, and it became evident that additional expense must be incurred before the enterprise could be made profitable.

At this period, a great flood swept the valley. All industry was at an end for the time. This was in the winter of 1862, known as the great season of floods. The miners were starved out. Professor Durant lost all he had invested in his mill. In the meantime, public attention was attracted to other discoveries, and thus the Gold Range was temporarily abandoned...

[Note: The last section of Browne's article discussed "The Iron Mountain," and the "Importance of Iron in Nevada," and "Copper, Silver, etc.," which did not specifically pertain to this review of the places along the East Walker River.]

———————

The Walker River Country
by J. Ross Browne
(Harper's New Monthly Magazine, Vol. 31, Issue 186, November 1865)
http://www.nevadaobserver.com/Walker%20River%20Country.htm

Browne's article that appeared in *Harper's New Monthly Magazine* may be accessed using the above website URL, courtesy of nevadaobserver.com.

Index

Creitzer, Mary (Mrs.), 57
Crummer, Harry Jackson (Jack), 90
Crummer, J. D., 88
Cumberland Coal Mining District, 69, 70
Cumberland mine, Coal Valley, 71

Dangberg ranch, Carson Valley, 57
Dangberg, Fred, 18, 34
Dangberg, Juanita (Mrs.), 18
Daniels, Agnes (nee McKeand), 93
Daniels, John, 93
Daniels, John C., 93
Daniels, Mary Jane, 93
Dayton, Nevada, 154
Dead 'Coon Beach, 39
Dempsey, Mamie, 20
Dibble, June (Mrs. A. S. Murphy), 91
Dixon, Mr., 2
Dixon's ranch, Esmeralda County
    (Dickinson's), 73
Doyle, Paddy, 89
Dressler, W. F., 18
Dreyer, Herman L., 127
Dryer, Herman, 127
Dulin, Kate (Mrs.), 45
Dulin, Theodora, 45
Dunlap, C. J., 154
Durand, Rev. Henry, 132
Durand's Mill, 142
Durand's Mills, 137
Durands Mills, 137
Durant, Henry, 143
Durant, Professor, 139
Durant's mill, 138
DURANT'S MILL, 131, 144, 148
Durant's mill site, 142
Durants Quatz [sic] Mill, 138
Durbin, Susan, 119
Dutch Bob (Rabb), 153

E. Walker Ranch, 109
Eagle Point, Mineral City, 148, 165
East Mason Valley Precinct, Lyon
    County, 63
East Walker, i, ii, iii, 1, 4, 5, 13, 30, 56,
    62, 64, 76, 83, 93, 95, 101, 107, 124,
    135
East Walker ranch, 109
East Walker Ranch, 112

East Walker Ranches, 87, 88, 112
East Walker river, 19, 95, 108, 122
East Walker River, i, ii, iii, 1, 4, 5, 13,
    21, 23, 25, 27, 42, 48, 58, 60, 62, 79,
    80, 101, 106, 116, 118, 122, 124,
    135, 137, 145, 151
East Walker River district, 59
East Walker River Mining, 145
East Walker River Mining and
    Agricultural Company, 146
East Walker River Mining District,
    138, 145
East Walker River Valley, 81, 138,
    146, 147
East Walker river, toll road on, 73
East Walker River, Walker River
    Mining District, 137
East Walker valley, 66
Eckis, Roland, 126
Eckis, Rollin P., 126
Eclipse ledge, Washington District, 75
Ede, Hattie S. (Mrs.), 56
Edward Shimmins, 116
Elbow Jack, 5
Elbow Jacks, 10
Elbow Jake, 5
Elbow Joe, 5, 6
Elbow Joe hill, 6
Elbow ranch, 21
Elbow Ranch, iii, 1, 2, 3, 4, 5, 6, 7, 9,
    11, 12, 13, 14, 15, 16, 18, 21, 22, 23,
    27, 31, 54, 55, 69, 75, 132, 133, 138,
    146
Elbow Ranch, toll-house at, 3
Elbow station, 12
Elbow Station, 5, 9, 12, 15
Elbow, Esmeralda County, Nevada, 11
Elbow, The, 4, 13
Emmet Vineyard, El Dorado County,
    10
Empire City, Nevada, 150
Esmeralda County Board of
    Commissioners, 4
Esmeralda Mining District, 131, 150
Esmeralda road, 2
Executive Order (Hot Springs), 42

Fagan, Peter (Fagin), 117
Fallon ranch, 102
Fallon, Catherine (death of), 102

Fallon, Delbert, 103
Fallon, Franklin, 103
Fallon, Ira, 102
Fallon, Ira (of Wellington), 108
Fallon, Ira (ranch), 84, 103, 110
Fallon, Ira Jr., 102, 103
Fallon, Ira T., 109
Fallon, Leland, 103
Fallon, Lucille, 102
Fallon, Milton E., 103
Farmers & Merchants National Bank, 162
Farmers Bank of Carson Valley, Inc., 163
Farwell, Isaac, 121
Farwell, Isaac N., 118
Farwell, Wealthy (Welthy) Paul, 119
Finney, L. C., 106
Finney, Lew C., 107
Fish, Amos, 82
Fish, Amos Fish (suicide of), 82
Fish, Amos Jr., 82
Fish, Mina E. (Amina Elizabeth), 82
Fish, Mina Elizabeth, 83
Fish, Nate, 94
Five Mile House, 4, 7, 48
Five Mile Ranch, 70, 73
Five-mile cañon, 48
Flat Creek Ranch, Humboldt County, Nevada, 90
Fleischmann Foundation, Max C., 86
Fleischmann, Charles L., 85
Fleischmann, Julius, 85
Fleischmann, Max, 84, 89, 98, 99, 103, 110
Fleischmann, Maximilian Charles, 85
Fleischmann, Sarah Hamilton, 85
Fleishman, Max C., 87
Fleishmann, Max C., 88
Fletcher, 48, 102
Fletcher Station, 7
Fletcher's, 12
Flying M Ranch, 68, 91
Flying-M Ranch, 91
Forbush, Elmer, 127
Forbush, Harry (Mr. and Mrs.), 127
Fort Churchill, 136, 153
Fossil beds, 66, 110
Franktown, mill at, 76
Franktown, Nevada, 154

Fraternal Cemetery, Wadsworth, Nevada, 14
Fryer Cattle Company, 165
Fryer Cattle Company, Charles M., 165
Fryer, Charles, 165

Gardner, Mr., 71
Gardner's Ranch, 72
General Grant Mining Company, 9
Genoa snow slide (1882), 34
Genoa, Douglas County, 34
George, Carrie, 22
George, Cassie, 22
George, Ida, 19
George, Mamie, 19
Gignoux ranch, 162, 163
Gignoux Ranch (Old), 164
Gignoux, Jules E., 162
Gignoux, May L., 162
Gilman, Charles, 116
Gilman, Charles (Virginia City), 116
Girgin, D. W., 35
Given, William, 69
Glann, Mrs., 152
Glazier property, 60
Glazier, Jack, 59, 61
Glazier, James, 61
Glazier, Jimmie, 59
Glazier, John H., 59, 61
Glazier, Sadie, 59
Glazier, Sadie Sam, 61
Glazier, William, 61
Glenbrook, Nevada, 86
Gold Cañon, Utah Territory, 54
Gold Hill Range, 139
Goldfield, 36
Governor James G. Scrugham, 110
Granite Bluff (Durant's Mill visible from), 141
Granite City, East Walker River, 132
Grant Mountain, 157
Grant View Hot Springs, 42
Gray, W. D., 35
Green (ranch), 84, 103, 110
Green Ranch, 87
Green, Amos, 14
Green, August, 15
Green, Augustus W., 15
Green, Everett A., 15

Lapham, W. W., 9, 55
Lapon Canyon, 157
Lapon Meadows, 157
Larson, George Virgil and Bernice, 88
Larson, Virgial (Mr. and Mrs., 112
Lash, Abram Jr., 50
Latapie ranch, 125
Latapie, Peter, 124, 127
Latapie, Pierre, 124
Latapie, Pierre (death), 124
Latapie, Pierre (Peter), 124
Laughlin, William R., 28
Lawson's Ford, 81, 147
Lawson's Ranch, 81, 147
Leavitt, Sybil, 14
Lee, William R., 10
Lewis Ranch, 88
Lewis ranch, Harry, 65
Lewis, Annetta, 78
Lewis, David J., 45, 154
Lewis, H. O., 59, 83
Lewis, Harry, 78
Lewis, Harry (Mr. and Mrs.), 102
Lewis, Harry O., 95
Lewis, John T., 6
Lewis, Lucille, 102
Litser property, Smith Valley,
    Nevada, 99
Livingston, John, 101
Livingston, Kate, 101
Log cabin, at Hot Spring, 40
Lookout Mountain, two miles above
    Mineral City, 118
Lucky Boy, Nevada, 83
Lufkin, D. T., 116
Lufkin, Lake & Co., 117
Lyon County, 20
Lyons and Welburn's bridge, across
    Walker river, 73
Lyons, R., 73

Mack & Green, Reno, 16
Mack, Charles E., 15
Mammoth mine, Coal Valley, 71
Manson, P., 152
Marshe's House, 3
Marsh's house, 134
Masini, Ida, 63
Masini, Lawrence, 63
Mason house, old, 160

Mason Valley, iii
Mason Valley Civilian Conservation
    Camp (CCC), 164
Mason Valley Soil Conservation
    Service, Yerington, 112
Mason Valley, Nevada, 152, 154
Mason, B., 152
Mason's Ranch, (N.H.A.), 152
Mathew's Ranch, 65
Mathews place, Joe, 56, 64
Mathews, Alfred, 64
Mathews, Annie, 64
Mathews, Antone, 64
Mathews, J., 62
Mathews, J. R., 62
Mathews, Joe, 59, 64
Mathews, Jose C., 64
Mathews, Joseph, 64
Mathews, Maria, 64
Mathews, William, 65
Matthews, Joe, 62
Matthews, Joseph R., 65
Maule, William M., 78, 164
May, Tom, 6
McCann, Ed, 21
McCann, Mamie Dempsey, 21
McConnell, Edward, 84, 103, 110
McDaniels, Mrs. V. B., 95
McInnis, Clara Morgan Boerlin, 38, 83
McInnis, Guy A., 38, 83
McKeough, John, 30, 101
McKeough, Julia C., 101
McKeough, Walter, 20
McKeough, Walter J., 30
McLane, A., 52
McLeod, Belle, 163
McTarnahan Toll Road, 106
McTarnahan, J. C., 106
Midway Resort, Aurora, Nevada, 59
Miller Hotel, Hawthorne, 37
Miller, John H., 36
Miller, William, 54
Mineral City, 145
Mineral City (Esmeralda County), 144
Mineral City, Esmeralda County,
    State of Nevada (Map of), 145
Mineral County Hospital, 30
Mineral County Library, Nevada, 87
Mineral County Museum, Nevada, 87
Mineral Hot Springs, 41

Perry district, 127
Peterson, Martin, 15
Peterson, Nelson, 15
Peterson's House, 15, 39
Pfister, Kate, 34
Pickett, Ollie (Mrs.), 57
Pierce, C. C. and Eileen E., 88
Pine Creek Mill Co., 117
Pine Grove Cemetery, Lyon County,
    Nevada, 120
Pine Grove District, 74, 117
Pine Grove school, 152
Pine Grove to Washington road", 105
Pine Grove Township, Esmeralda
    County, 15
Pine Grove, Nevada, 54, 82, 83, 93,
    152, 154
Pine Grove, Rockland Township,
    Esmeralda County, 14
Pine, D. H., 159
Pioneer mill, The (Wheeler's), 152
Plymouth Rock (piece of), 146
Point of Rocks, East Walker River, 58
Poli ranch, 97
Poli Ranch, 100, 102
Poli, Arthur, 102
Poli, Daniel E., 101
Poli, Della, 101
Poli, Della M., 101
Poli, Mrs. Nelson (death of), 101
Poli, Nelson, 95, 100, 108
Poli, Nelson (death and burial), 102
Poli, Nelson (estate of), 102
Polie, Nelson, 100
Polli Ranch [sic], 87
Polli's (sic) ranch, 95
Polli's House, 100
Polly (Poli) (ranch), 84, 103, 110
Poor, Willie, 6
Powell Ranch, 105
Powell's House, 105
Pray, 117
President Theodore Roosevelt, 43
Pritchard, Guy, 45
Pritchard, Thomas B., 45
prospect shaft for coal, 50
Pugh, J. W., 2
Pugh, John W., 73

Quartz Mill, furnace stack in old, 149

Quartz Mill, Old, 149, 158

Rabe (Dutch Bob), 153
Rabinell, Z. (Ravenelle), 27
Raccoon Beach, 39
Rafter 7 Ranch, 127, 162
Rafter Seven Ranch House, 128
Ravanelle, Eusebe B., 27
Ravanelle, Nancy, 27
Ravanelle, Willie, 27
Ravenel Ranch, 31, 32
Ravenell, Eusebe, 27
Ravenell, John A., 27
Ravenell, Nancy, 27
Ravenell, Zeb, 27
Ravenelle and Pine Grove Road, 58
Ravenelle Ditch, East Fork, 27
Ravenelle ranch, 30
Ravenelle to Pine Grove Road, 37
Ravenelle, Eusebe B., 25
Ravenelle, Mrs., 30
Ravenelle, Nancy, 27
Ravenelle, Philina, 28
Ravenelle, Phillini N., 28
Ravenelle, Z. B., 25, 26, 27, 29
Ravenelle, Z. B. (death and burial), 29
Ravenelle, Zeb, 29, 35
Ravenelle, Zebe, 28
Ravnals, Zebedee (Ravenelle), 27
Ravnelle's House, 25
Ravnelles House, 32
Rawhide, town of, 160
Red, White and Blue mine, Aurora,
    117
Richards, W. A. (Commissioner,
    General Land Office), 42
Riley, Mr., 69
Robinson and Co., A. D., 120
Robinson, A., 120
Robinson, A. D. and S. A., 120
Robinson, Alice Maria, 120
Robinson, Amos D., 120
Robinson, Amos D. (Postmaster, Pine
    Grove), 122
Robinson, Ida M., 123
Robinson, Richard, 119, 121
Robinson, Richard and Susan, 120
Robinson, S., 122
Robinson, Sarah, 120
Robinson, Susan, 122, 123

Robinson, Susan Durbin, 119
Robinson, Susan Maria, 119
Robinson, Susan, widow of Richard
    Robinson, 123
Robinson, W., 120
Robinson, Walter, 120
Rodi, Carl D., 126
Rodi, Earl, 126
Roosevelt, Theodore (President), 43
Rosaschi Ranch, 164
Rosaschi ranch, old, 165
Rosaschi, Ambro, 31, 162, 163
Rosaschi, Ambro Sr. (death of), 164
Rosaschi, Ambro, Jr., 163
Rosaschi, Belle, 163
Rosaschi, Helen, 163
Rosaschi, Idele, 163
Rosaschi, Mrs. Connie, 102
Rosaschi, Romeo, 162
Ross, E. J., 66
Rough Creek, 89
Rough Creek (toll road from), 9
Rowe ranches, 165
Rowe, William, 165

S. F. Trust and Mining Company, 132,
    144
Salas Ranch [sic] (Salles Ranch), 127
Salles ranch, 126, 127
Salles, Bertrand, 124, 127
Salles, Bertrand (death), 124
Salt Lake City, Utah Territory, 150
Sam, Bill, 59
Sam, Mattie, 59
Santa Gertrudis cattle, 90, 91
Santa Margarita ranch, 165
Santa Margarita Ranch, 162, 165
Sayre, Andrew P., 8
Sayre, Mrs. A. P., 8
Sayre, Sophia H. (Mrs.), 8
Schreck brothers, 9
Schreck, Frank, 8, 9
Schreck, Henry, 8
Schreck, Herman, 8
Schreck, Infant, 7
Schreck, J., 7
Schreck, Joe, 5
Schreck, Joseph, 5, 8, 9
Schreck, Mrs. J., 8
Schreck, Mrs. Jos., 8

Schreck, O. A., 7
Schreck, Sophia (Mrs.), 8
Schultze, F. W., 5
Schurz Paiute Indian Cemetery, 21
Scrivner, Benjamin and Talitha, 158
Scrivner, Susan A., 155
Scrugham, James G. (Governor), 110
Seawell, Judge (W. M.), 155
Sharpe Ranch (Fletcher), 102
Shedd, George, 6
Sherlock, J. C. (Mr. and Mrs.), 85
Sherlock, Sarah Hamilton, 85
~~Sherman~~ Durants Quatz [sic] Mill,
    138
Sherman, A. G., 115, 117, 138
Sherman, A. G. (East Walker River),
    116
Sherman, Albert Gallatin, 116
Sherman, E. A., 146
Sherman, E. A. (Major), 48
Sherman, Edwin A., 73, 144
Sherman, Major, 146
Shermans Ranch, 115
Shimman, Robert (fire loss), 122
Shimmen's Ranch, 118, 140
Shimmin or Robinson ranch, 124
Shimmin ranch, 124
Shimmin Ranch, 108, 118, 126, 138,
    149, 154
Shimmin, Annie W., 110
Shimmin, Annie Webster, 108
Shimmin, Bertha, 123
Shimmin, E. R., 108
Shimmin, Edward R., 119, 120, 122,
    123
Shimmin, Edward Robert, 119, 122
Shimmin, Francis, 119
Shimmin, Gracie, 123
Shimmin, R. L., 122
Shimmin, R. W., 122
Shimmin, Richard W., 119, 123
Shimmin, Robert E., 119, 122
Shimmin, Robert L., 108, 119, 122,
    123
Shimmin, Robert Larue, 122
Shimmin, Rosetta, 123
Shimmin, Sarah J., 119
Shimmin, Susan Robinson (death and
    burial), 119
Shimmin, Thomas W., 119